FA FOCUSED

YOUR SIMPLE FOUR-STEP GUIDE TO INTENTIONALLY CREATING YOUR BEST LIFE NOW

DR. TRANEIKA TURNER-WENTT

This book is dedicated to HOPE *for our future selves.*

TABLE OF CONTENT

Acknowledgements

Writing a book about the Principles that changed your life while also layering in it the story of how your life has been changed is a surreal experience. Staying committed to the process of turning an idea into a book is more complex than it seems. I eventually repurposed the reservations I had about releasing my sacred imprint into the world in the form of a book and found the grace to submit the final manuscript. I could not have done this without the encouragement, prayers and support of loved ones.

Michael D. Wentt, my husband, the philosopher, your love has lifted me higher than I've ever been lifted before. Our lives and our stories aligned for such a time as this. Thank you for the thought provoking conversations and for putting up with the late night light from the laptop screen for months. I love you dearly.

Pearl (Mother), my dream girl, you have used your imagination in such a wonderful and life changing way. Thank you for always believing in me and cheering me on to the finish line and beyond each time I embark upon a new phase of my journey.

Horace (Dad), my first spiritual teacher, you've always told me that I can do anything I put my mind to, thank you for being so convincing. You always kept prayer at the forefront of our family life and the impact is undeniable.

Aunt Ola (Mamma V & Daddy J), your home was my first library, thanks for giving me access to all of those encyclopaedias and children's books. Aunts Anne & Faye thanks for asking about what's next on my journey. I pray that my answers have made you and my uncles proud.

Monique, thanks for being a sister-friend and for staying present through the frustrations and triumphs on my journey to authorship.

Qualaune, Faith, Ruth W., and Lamond sometimes a book is judged by its cover, thanks for validating the design.

DEAR READER

Becoming faithfully focused on the process of creating your best life now is like making travel plans. We all have desired to go someplace we have never been or back to a place we once loved and imagined what the experience would be like upon our arrival.

However, some people have never traveled outside of their immediate vicinity because their exposure to other locations is limited. They are simply unaware that there are other spaces and places that they may enjoy beyond what they have already experienced. They may even think that traveling to beautiful places is for other people and not them. It could also be that they have never taken the time to get a passport or they have a fear of flying or cruising. Regardless of what was standing between them and their desired destination, once they open up to new possibilities, the arrival to the destination seems to make everything they went through to get there worth it.

It can feel like being on a vacation when life presents us with an opportunity to step into a new version of ourselves, a new reality. Sometimes simply thinking of what it will be like to become a business executive, a parent, a homeowner, a spouse, or entrepreneur can be a much-needed vacation from our current reality. This vacation is like any other one, you have to consider your options and then take the necessary steps to get to the place you have chosen. Deciding where you want to go and dreaming about how great it's going to be once you get there can be momentarily as enjoyable as the vacation itself. It is the dreaming about getting there that motivates us to rent the vehicle, stand in the line at the travel center, or complete the application for a passport.

This book discusses the way to move forward using principles that every person with a purpose needs to know about focusing on their goals and aligning with the answer to their prayer. Get ready to pack up doubt about your worthiness to become a better version of yourself and drop it off in a place you'll soon see no reason to return to. You'll be too busy unpacking a different, more desirable set of circumstances as souvenir reminders of the beautiful places within yourself that you've recently visited. Life is definitely about the destination but it is also about the journey you take to get there. Faithfully Focused, presents opportunities for you to imagine where you want to go and provides you with an easy four-step plan to get there. In it, I share personal potholes, re-routes and a few perfect landings from my own journey in hopes of letting you know you're not alone on the road to your best life.

Faithfully,
Dr. Traneika Turner-Wentt

Intention + Attention = Invention
Dr. Traneika Turner-Wentt

Faith + Focus = The Future

Dr. Traneika Turner-Wentt

Preface

Much of our time in the present is spent thinking about our future goals. Somewhere between the thought and the reality of our dream come true, we lose faith. I believe this occurs because many of us don't know how to maintain our focus. As spiritual beings, we are taught a lot about faith and very little about focus. We have learned that faith is essential, but we think focus is optional. We listen to sermons on faith, read books on faith, and attend conferences about faith, but we shy away from learning to sustain our focus. One thing that we all know for sure is that faith is essential for manifesting the unseen substance of our desire into a tangible reality. However, we think it's questionable to compliment the transcendent element of faith with the cerebral component of focus. We feel that, somehow, we're cheating on our religion if we intentionally seek ways to augment it.

When our faith is no longer strong enough to fuel the fire of our deferred dream, we feel let down. After reading this book, you'll learn that focus is there as a springboard to help you bounce back into a better position.

After 20 years of dedication supporting people from a wide range of cultures, a core tenet of my personal and professional philosophy is that people desire better for themselves and those they love. Over the years, this work has revealed to me that faith alone does not bring us into alignment with our desired reality. If you are out of alignment in one area, you're probably also misaligned in other parts of your life. As I have gained greater insight into the areas of people's lives that bring them the most triumph or challenge I've categorized them into four life domains that I'll share with you as a part of the C.A.R.E. process.

I wanted to make it easy for you to remember these areas, so they too, have the C.A.R.E. acronym. Below are the four life domains as well as the definitions that I have used for each of them, in conjunction with Meriam Webster's Dictionary, of course.

The Domains

1. Co-Creative Consciousness – a state of realizing your connection to the Divine and your ability to influence your internal and external reality.
2. Assets – a valuable, flourishing or thriving person, thing, or quality, especially in financial respects, good fortune.
3. Relationship – the way in which two or more people are interconnected or regard and behave toward each other.
4. Empowerment – the quality or state of being healthy in body and mind, especially as the result of a deliberate process. A state of mental, physical, and social well-being.

As a heart-mind transformation method, C.A.R.E. is an inspiring way to move yourself from where you are now to where you desire to be. Within the pages of this book exists foundational principles needed to help you as you are becoming your best self yet. This book is not technical. I purposely did not write a faith-based treatment handbook for clinical professionals. This book is hands-on; it is user-friendly and paints a personal portrait of your destination by design. The goal of this work is not theoretical; it is intended to impact the reader in a practical way.

The practical advice shared here will help you embrace a new method for how you maneuver through the unchartered terrain in your life. As you advance through this book, please make the internal commitment to creating the results you desire in a manner that is aligned with your highest and greatest good. Read this book entirely and more than once. It is here to support you no matter where you are on the journey to your best life.

I believe that in life there is only one destination, and it is to the best possible version of you. We are all capable of evolving into something greater than we are now. Whether or not we choose to ever become our healthiest, wealthiest, happiest, most conscious self is entirely up to us. I am asking you, right now, to shift your perspective. I invite you to create your biggest and brightest vision for your future. You are invited to reach further and grab more than you ever imagined possible. You are encouraged to see yourself living in the midst of your desired reality. Your journey begins the moment you set your intention. Beyond this page is a roadmap to get to where you know in your heart you are meant to be.

Introduction
to Focus

Focus is a neurological skill that allows us to maintain our attention on a task and direct our efforts, without procrastination, until the task is complete. Life offers no shortage of distractions. We are easily and frequently taken off course by notifications and alerts about what we need to do next. If you're trying to focus on one thing, another thing needs your attention. Sometimes, just knowing there is more to do, even when we're not doing it, can build anxiety and diminish our ability to concentrate on the task at hand. Complex tasks require patience. Individuals with a more resilient and long lasting attention span have an advantage, over those who do not possess those qualities, for producing better outcomes in their lives.

Focusing without distraction on a responsibility as cognitively demanding as fulfilling your purpose, is deep work. It is not surprising that such work has been commonly delegated to examination within the context of religious activity.

Dealing with distractions is difficult brain work and it can be mitigated by engaging in focused activity. The benefits of having a go-to-plan for staying focused significantly increases your ability to filter out irrelevant stimuli.

Invitation to Focus

I have dedicated much of my personal and professional time to doing the most exciting work imaginable: helping others identify and remove their roadblocks. As you navigate through this book and more importantly your life, I invite you to come to the center of purpose and meaning, where the road is clearer. In other words, this is an invitation to get focused on what really matters to you. But why focus? The very thought of it may bring up memories of getting a headache from concentrating too long on the solution to a difficult problem. My intent is to help you unfold the rich rewards of infusing faith with focus.

What keeps people from being faithfully focused? I have thought long and hard about that, and here is my conclusion. They haven't been encouraged to create daily habits that support their spiritual and mental connectivity to their desired destination, their dreams. Connecting to our dreams can be one of the happiest or saddest times of our lives. Dreaming of the life we want to live can create such happiness; however, looking back on unfulfilled wishes can be sad. Are you happy, fulfilled and living your best life now? If so, you have achieved something uncommon. This is why I have written this book, to help more people connect with their best life by creating daily neuro-spiritual habits that keep them on course to reach their desired destination.

It is in paying attention to your desires that you breathe life into them and they manifest. You are the generator of your very own happiness, and it is high time for you to believe in your future possibilities. After all, knowing that all things are possible should give you hope and inspire you to take action toward the future that you believe is possible. But wait, you say, "I used to believe, and I didn't get what I wanted." As a social scientist, I have found that as good, purpose-filled people, we often turn to religion to bring us the solutions to why we have what we have and are where we are now. As a result of these questions, many feel as though there is a problem with the Creator (God doesn't love me) or a problem with themselves (I'm not worthy) as the reason they are where they are now instead of where they desire to be. Nothing could be further from the truth. I do, however, understand your plight, and I'm here to help.

Focus in Action

I have spent tens of thousands of hours changing the lives of people in individual, couples, and family therapy. My clients recommend me to others due to the results they achieve with me. While I was always happy that my clients achieved great success, the scientific investigator in me repeatedly posed one lingering question about what made transformation easier for some than others.

The same question applied to me. I had attained great results in most domains in my life, while it took years beyond what I thought was reasonable to achieve it in another area. So I began to look beyond what I had learned in the educational and religious institutions to which I was affiliated. Caveat, my spiritual upbringing is the foundation for who I am as an individual, and my educational background has also served me well. Nonetheless, more than a decade ago, I learned about the law of attraction. One day I *happened* to be home from work early due to attending a training; I walked in and turned on the television, which *happened* to be tuned to The Oprah Winfrey Show. At that moment, she was discussing how a book changed her life. It was near the end of the show, so I didn't catch much else, but I hurried to write down the name of the book and purchased it shortly after. I remember opening it, and based on the title, I thought the information would be similar to what I had been taught in Sunday School.

That's when things got complicated because it had a somewhat religious tone to which I was familiar, and because it also explained the meaning behind so many scriptural references, I was quite intrigued. It was puzzling how I had been around this information since I was a young girl sitting in the pews of many church services but had never heard it described with such clarity and seeming accuracy. Well, I absorbed every drop dripped from the pages of that book and began to apply it to my own life. Considering that the language of the book seemed to run parallel to my own internal knowing, it was not a challenge to wrap my mind around it at all. Before I knew it, I had combined it with other popular methods that were consistent with my spiritual values such as affirmations, emotional freedom

> "The greatest discovery of all time is that a person can change his future by merely changing his attitude."
> *Oprah Winfrey*

technique, ho'oponopono, etc. much of which brought about desirable outcomes, though not the authentic manifestations for which I had hoped. After seeing success with a wide range of clients, my inner scientist inherently knew that there was a methodical way to construct a desirable future.

After more than a decade of independently studying principles that govern the universe, one day, I was guided to write down the method that I used with clients and start a podcast on the power of intention. Following this guidance allowed me to clearly see the commonalities between the spiritual laws, the scientific method, and the social environment that make manifesting our desires attainable. I now had a firmer foundation upon which to build the neuro-spiritual framework offered here. Since then, I have continued to help set clients on the path to focus on their dreams and get more intentional about what they desire in their lives.

Unintentionally, using this framework to get clear on my desire, helped set me on the path to meet my amazing husband. I'll also be sharing my own personal story of how I used the advice offered here.

This book is written for anyone who desires more insight on how we get what we get in life as well as for the person who desires to experience change in any area of life without leaving it to chance.

You must do your part though to move through the turbulence of uncertainty with confidence and grace. What is your part, you ask? You must believe. You must believe beyond any doubt. You must believe beyond any doubt to the contrary. You must believe beyond any doubt to the contrary that you already are and already have the manifestation of your desire. You must move from your current state of being to the place in time that your desire exists before it physically manifests. When you do this, your thoughts and actions begin to align with your intentional focus, and you start to live in the zone of manifested miracles, or what I like to call the *delivery zone*. I know it stretches your emotional intellect when you have to consider already being what you desire to become; but plain and simple, that is what you must do to get into the delivery zone.

The delivery zone explained

When you go online to order that much-needed item, at the end of your order, you are asked for your billing address, and separately, you are asked for your shipping address. The billing address is the physical location of the person placing and paying for the order. The shipping address is the address where you desire your order to be delivered in the future. As you will learn from this book, you are in a constant state of change; hence, where you are now is not the same place you will be in the future, mentally or physiologically. The time between the order and the delivery is there to allow you to encounter people, places, and things that move you to the location of your delivery. For example, if your desire is to find a romantic partner, if you ask for a person who is a great time manager, and you are a person who is always late, then after you make your request you will encounter situations that are designed to make you a timelier person, like the person you are asking for. As I will say in many different ways throughout this book, like attracts like.

Like attracts like

Do you remember the elementary school experiment with the tuning forks, where you ding one and all the other ones in the room with a matching frequency start to ring along with it? This also happens with our thoughts. The more you think about something, the more you begin to attract everything on the level of what you're thinking about. This is why the saying, 'when it rains, it pours' rings true. One cloudy, wet situation attracts another, and that one attracts another one, and so on, until you're standing in a muddy puddle of like situations. The good news is that you can decide not only to know that behind those clouds the sun is shining somewhere but to also see its rays peeking out to dry up the muddy water beneath your feet. Let me assure you that starting with one thought that makes you feel better about the situation is enough to get those clouds moving from over your head. A simple way to think better-feeling thoughts is to read or listen to something inspirational that raises your vibration. Nourishing your mind with inspirational information is vital to accelerating the arrival of your desired outcome.

Neuro-spirituality

I am confident that spirituality is a companion to science, not its competitor. The Creator skillfully intertwined science, sociology, and spirituality into all of creation, and this intent can be witnessed throughout the Universe. For example, human beings can be explained scientifically using anatomy,

"Science without religion is lame, religion without science is blind."
Albert Einstein

biology, and physiology. There is also a sociological component to our existence that drives most beings to desire to be a part of a community such as family, friendships, and organizations. Lastly, the part of us that desires to live out our purpose through connection to a Higher Power is spiritual.

It is safe to say that no one group understands all there is to know about the scientific and spiritual workings of the Universe. The time has come for thought leaders in the scientific and spiritual community to uncover the commonalities between each field, acknowledge the correlations, and disseminate a message of unity between the two. This book places you ahead of the learning curve as these disciplines fully converge to allow a more complete understanding of our world and how it works to unfold our desired reality. The emerging multidisciplinary field of neuro-spirituality is leading the way. Yale University researchers have confirmed that there is a place in our brains that processes spiritual experiences[1]. Finding this neurobiological home for spirituality further proves that humans are hardwired for it. This book takes a neuro-spiritual approach to help you use faith (spirituality) and focus (neuro-science) to becoming all that you desire to be. Faithfully Focused is meant to be a simple handbook, which easily and efficiently synthesizes the processes related to the power you have, to co-create your reality. Yes, you. On my personal journey of creation and manifestation, I have discovered that I am a co-creator with the Creator, that there is a methodical intelligence and a spiritual force simultaneously working to make us much more powerful than we know. I have learned that integrating the scientific method does not diminish the authority of the spiritual forces, but rather, science is driven by the invisible spiritual world, and the two are more effective together than apart.

A discussion on the way our desires manifest would be incomplete without showing you how to use your head (focus) and your heart (faith) in the process; this is referred

> When following your heart, be sure to take your brain with you.

to as neuro-faith. Failure to understand this combination is one reason that some self-help methods are not useful beyond a seminar with a motivational speaker. Many books are conceptual at best, they offer information that stimulates the mind or methods that engage the heart; seldom do you find a book, such as this one, that integrates both the head and the heart, focus and faith, into the conceptual framework and the manifestation method. Don't stop reading now; this book invites you beyond visualizations or verbalization of affirmations to a place of integrating a simple heart-mind method called C.A.R.E.; to easily and efficiently move you into the delivery zone. Using this method will help you bring about a change in your mindset through faithfully focusing on your desired outcome. Remember, change has to occur in your mind before it happens in your reality.

"What you think about, you bring about."
Rhonda Byrne

Measuring the Miles

How far do we have to go?

How many times have you known what to do and still not taken action to do it? If you're like millions of people, then the answer is probably, plenty. We all have known what to do regarding a change we needed to make numerous times and not taken the steps to do it. This is because we need more than information to create lasting change in our lives. For example, brush your teeth after each meal, consistently, and you will avoid a cavity. Simple, right? We learn to brush our teeth at a young age, yet millions of people have cavities because they do not follow this simple instruction consistently. For too long, most of us have believed that change has to be complicated; however, the key to creating change is consistency.

> "Change will not come if we wait for some other person or some other time. We are the change we have been waiting for. We are the change which we seek."
> *Barak Obama*

How many times has reading a book about a problem resolved your issue? If you're anything like the masses, then the answer is, probably, not many. There is no worthy substitute for action; you must take the necessary action steps to reach your destination. Acquiring knowledge alone is like throwing a handful of apple seeds in the wind and expecting them to land, take root, and grow into beautiful apple trees yielding delicious fruit. What is the likelihood of that happening? You got it, not likely. Take affirmations, for instance, saying an affirmation is like introducing new information (seeds) to your mind (soil). However, research suggests that individuals with low-self-esteem (weeds) were found to feel worse after repeating positive affirmations (delicious apples) alone. You might think it is not possible to eat delicious apples and feel worse after doing so; after all, apples are nutritious and taste good too. When a person's taste buds are only programed for junk food, then that person's misalignment with healthy food convinces them that they actually feel bad after eating apples. For instance, if a person who desires to be married repeats, "I have a spouse who loves me." while they are actually wondering "Will I ever go on a date again?" they are likely feel worse. This is why affirmations about the end results don't work at the beginning of your manifestation journey. Affirmations work best after you have conditioned your heart to believe and your mind to receive the outcome you are affirming.

Delivery zone tip: *create affirmations that are in sync with where you are on your journey. At the beginning of your journey to obtain your desired result, you can affirm that 'having' that specific result is good. It can be as simple as stating – having more income is good, having better health is good, having a loving relationship is good.*

Forget what you have heard, you have the ability to create anything that you truly desire and live a more fulfilled and purposeful life as a result of your very own faithful focus.

When you stand in your power as a co-creator with the Creator, your personal platform rises to meet you. When you become in mind who you see yourself to be in Spirit, things and people around you begin to align and even assist with your endeavors. The work of God is accomplished through people, and when you stay focused, you are guaranteed to cross paths with those who are placed there to assist you with becoming all that you were purposed to be. Just as, one day, you will be the person who assists someone else. I know you may be wondering, why is it that you encounter people who seem to directly oppose the fulfillment of your desire, causing chaos and delay on your journey to manifesting the good you desire to see in your life? I'm glad you asked. Nothing helps you clarify the details of your desire better than an encounter with its opposite.

T-time: During a time of transformation, I was conducting an inventory of the people in my life. Thankfully, I have been fortunate to keep the company of honest, respectable, fun-loving people; however, there was an area that I noticed was primarily filled with very pessimistic people. I thought I was placed among those individuals to be 'a light,' when the truth was, I was there to see hidden thoughts being reflected back to me.

One day, while listening to a podcast, the speaker said that if you notice any area in your life where you are surrounded by negative people, then that means you are matching their negative energy. Now that got my antennas up because although I

"The cause of all expansion is awareness; the cause of any dilemma is ignorance."
Bob Proctor

was usually deemed to be the eternal optimist, I knew there had to be some truth to vibing on their level. Before changing my perspective, I frequently thought about and discussed the aspects of the project that I did not like, such as the poor attitudes of the team members. However, after listening to that speaker, I immediately stopped verbalizing what I didn't like and ramped up my positive outlook whenever I was in that environment. Within a few months' time, my assignment on the project ended, and I was asked to lead a different initiative. One that was considerably more aligned with my intention. This further solidified my inner knowing that like attracts like. Although I saw myself as a generally upbeat person, having this happen reminded me how vital it is to take inventory of my thoughts to be certain that they are aligned with my desires.

C.A.R.E. is an acronym for: Characterize, Appreciate, Requisition, and Engage. The C.A.R.E. Framework is a neuro-spiritual method designed to help you faithfully focus on your desired future. Using this method will allow you to change your focus so you can faithfully construct your future.

If you continue to read this book and implement the tools provided here – that will teach and show you how placing your focus onto the things you desire is the way to achieve your life's dreams — you will start to notice a change immediately.

You'll start to experience a shift, and the more you focus on what you desire and the purpose for having it, the faster it will begin to manifest for you. Focus is like a spotlight, illuminating the object of our attention.

What are you waiting for? It's time to change your focus and start constructing the future you've always dreamed about. No more procrastination. No more excuses. No more delays.

> A year from now, you'll wish you had started today.

Let's get started!

ACTION STEP:

Thought Inventory

State your desire: My desire is
_____.

What thoughts are aligned with this desire? List each thought.

How often do you think this thought? Daily_____
Weekly_____

CHAPTER 1

WHERE I DESIRE TO BE

Are we there yet?

You may be thinking, shouldn't I be "there" by now? Doing what I desire to do with my life, being what I desire to be, already having those much-anticipated experiences. One of the best questions to ask yourself at

> "Without a vision for the future, we reconstruct the past."
> *Dr. Traneika Turner-Wentt*

this juncture is do I have a clear vision of what I desire to see in my life?

Unfortunately, many people do not know what they desire or why, and they are busy working toward goals that are misaligned with their personal values.

They are subconsciously sending signals into the Universe that do not appropriately reflect their authentic purpose in life.

Let me share some insight into how this happens. Our prayers go out into the heavens in the form of thoughts and feelings. They attract back to us matter (people, places, things) that cause us to feel the way we felt when we sent them out. This point would be more easily demonstrated if the universe immediately sent back matter matching our thoughts, thankfully, it doesn't (can you imagine thinking of a pink elephant and having it instantly appear?). But because of time, we have misread the principle of sowing and reaping or the law of cause and effect as it relates to our thoughts and feelings. Until now it probably wasn't clear to you that your thoughts, feelings, and behaviors determine your circumstances.

You have often seen or heard the phrase "change your thoughts, change your life," and this is a noble and true statement indeed. When you learn to master your thoughts, and more importantly, your feelings, you can surely change any situation from intangible to tangible or from destitute to desirable. This is how it works.

Every time you think a thought, emit an emotion, or take an action, certain neural pathways in the brain get activated. Taking the same action, feeling the same emotion, or thinking the same thought strengthens that particular neural pathway by making it thicker and deeper. Over time, new pathways go from being like the thin flimsy vein of a leaf to more like the roots of a mature oak tree deeply embedded in the neural network of the brain.

For example, when you take a new, unfamiliar route to the store, at first, it is a very conscious effort. You are looking at your surroundings, watching for changes in the road. However, after you have taken that path several times, the nuances of the route become so embedded in your brain that navigating it becomes a subconscious effort. Meaning that you don't dedicate your full conscious attention to it; it becomes a program in the background and frees up your mind to focus on the dinner party you're planning while listening to an audiobook. This is the exact same process that allows a person who perfects the practice of a sport daily to become an Olympic medalist, or a person who always notices what's wrong to become a chronic pessimist. These internal programs, created by habits, are silently running in the background, and we subconsciously rely on them each time we make a choice[2]. And as you know, our lives are made up of the choices that we make, so essentially, our subconscious programming dictates our lives.

To close the gap between where you are now and the actions you take to get where you desire to be, you need subconscious programming that is aligned with your desired destination. Look at it like this, you desire to visit the sunny beaches of California; however, your GPS is programmed to go to Florida, which also has sunshine and beaches. If you follow the guidance of your GPS, then you will be directed to a place other than your desired destination. Although the route may have been lined with sand and water, upon your arrival, you might ask, how did I get here? Similar to this, if your desired destination is to be married and you believe that being married is too challenging, you read every gossip report about failed marriages, and you tell yourself love is too risky, then your subconscious program is going to be misaligned with your desired destination of being happily married. Because of the misaligned programming as the source of your decision making, you are more likely to make choices that will lead you to face challenges and engage in activities that eventually cause you to fail at being married. After reading this example, you should easily see the importance of aligning your thoughts with your desired outcome.

Delivery zone tip: *Inspect your internal GPS to ensure it is programmed for where you desire to go.*

ACTION STEP:

Which thoughts from your past or especially your present do you need to realign with where you desire to go?

CHAPTER 2

WHERE I AM NOW

How did I get here?

Have you ever wondered how you got what you have in life? Or how someone was promoted over you? And my personal favorite, how did she get married and not me?

> "Your focus is your reality."
> *Yoda*

The latter being a question I was still asking myself after having been proposed to twice by two different very successful and eligible men in my 20s and 30s before later meeting and marrying my husband. Wanting to be a wife and thinking of yourself as a wife are two different things, each thought yielding its own result. So be mindful of what you call yourself.

> **Delivery zone tip:** *be mindful of what you call others too because your inner self is listening to every word you say and making those words applicable to you.*

Watching Our Words – WOW Yourself

Ever heard the term 'word is bond?' Your words form a sacred bond with the Universe. Each word that you think and speak is bonded to a potential outcome. This is why the power of the word is unparalleled. In the beginning was the Word, and the Word frames the World.

Remember that your word is what calls your desire into existence. The word is the progenitor of any movement or substance in your life. Everything material that exists has a name, a word that describes its character. Words, thoughts, and things are interconnected. Words can be expressed mentally through thoughts, physically in writing, and orally through speech. Think about it, you can have a thought that only resides in your mind. When you write that thought on paper, then you have gotten it out of your head so that you can physically see it. The spoken word is powerful because it charges the atmosphere surrounding you as a combined expression of your mental and physical activity. The scripture tells us that faith comes by hearing. Have you ever noticed that people around you can see your good works, but at times, choose to believe a negative comment they heard about you in the absence of proof? This is because hearing is believing. The tongue is small, but it is mighty because it is powered by the strongest invisible force you have access to, your thoughts. It also has the power to influence the thoughts of others.

We know that thoughts create things and that those thoughts arise as a result of your mental focus. I will discuss the types of focus and why we need them in a future chapter. In the meantime, use your words and choose them wisely. Send those words into your future and expect to receive the delicious fruit they will produce. The 55th chapter of Isaiah verses 9-11, paint a clear picture of the Creator's thoughts being like rain and snow leaving the heavens, and instead of simply returning to the heavens the same way they left, each leaves the heavens and accomplishes its mission of watering the earth. This causes the recipients of this heaven-to-earth irrigation system to prosper. This analogy sets the framework for our understanding of the verses to follow, which explain the way that words leave the sender's mouth and prosper in the environment to which they were sent. If positive words were sent out, then positivity returns, likewise, if indifference was sent, then despair or doubt is what returns.

If you have access to my 90-day Faithfully Focused planner, then open it up and select a few random days for goodness to show up in your future. Highlight them, and then at the top of the space, write something like: "today was a great day," or "wow, that really made me happy today." The blank space between the lines is sacred and there to remind you that you have the freedom to creatively fill in your future as you envision it. You are the master of your destiny, no one else. It is your focus that co-creates your future, no one else's.

ACTION STEP:

Think about a time in the past when you sent out positive thoughts regarding a potentially negative situation and got a better outcome as a result.

Think about your current desire. Write a positive statement related to your desire.

Here is mine. My desire is to remodel my home with high-quality products at a low cost. My beautiful new sofa looks perfect in the family room; I purchased it for 40% off the sale price.

CHAPTER 3

CHANGE OF LOCATION

Location, location, location

We've all been on the road to a certain location and either turned around or stopped too soon at a different place because it was more convenient than continuing to the destination. Let's deal with changing your desire to fit your current location. Everyone comes across a stagnation that presents itself as a formidable opponent to the future they desire. Feeling stagnant and unfulfilled often leads people to redefine their desires based on their situation; to make themselves feel better about staying where they are now and settling for less. This causes us to accept where we are now as where we will always be, all the while, convincing ourselves that we are ok with it. Understand this, no matter what it has looked like, nothing from your past has more power than the Divine purpose ahead of you.

Where are you allowing what could have been a temporary stagnation to dictate your future situation? When we have unfulfilled desires or when the desires of our heart are not manifested, we feel a void. Take it from me, no undesirable situation is strong enough to defeat the power of your focus.

There are many reasons that we may ask for something and not get it, often, we say that it is not God's will. The Good Book says that it is the Father's good pleasure to give you the kingdom (Luke 12:32 KJV), and further tells us that no good thing will be withheld from those who walk on the right path (Psalm 84:11 KJV).

One thing that we must be clear about is that The Creator is not Lucy from the Peanuts Pod. The Most High does not beckon us hither promising us that this time is our time, and then move the ball or push the finish line back further than it was when we started. Now, if you consider yourself "good enough" to spend eternity with God, then you are "good enough" to receive the Kingdom of Heaven here on Earth.

Any doubters who believe that the reference of Kingdom is only related to unseen spiritual things, must refer to Matthew 7:11, which says, how much more shall your Father who is in heaven give good things to those who ask Him. Understanding this is vitally important to anyone who plans to ask God for anything. Since we know that thoughts precede things, you must first take on good thoughts toward yourself before expecting good things to come to you.

How do you ask God for a good thing? Yes, you, how do you currently ask God for something that you desire? Walk yourself through your process and write your response.

What did you notice? Did you notice that you ask for what you want by actually talking about what you don't want? "Well, I know I don't want a partner who is going to be unfaithful to me or someone who can't hold a decent conversation in a social situation."

Stop right there. It does not serve us to place our attention on anything that is not what we desire. Have you ever seen a person with blurred or double vision try to reach their destination? It can be painful to watch them walk into walls, bump their knee, or even miss their destination altogether. Double-mindedness will cause unnecessary delays and detours on your journey.

Trying to focus on what you desire while constantly thinking about what you do not want is like taking one step forward and two steps back. And you never know which one of these steps back will cause you to slide down the slippery slope of doubt, despair, or dependency upon someone else to make your dreams come true. So become single-minded, or, in other words, focus on your desires and watch the signs of their manifestation begin to show up.

That sign could be as simple as meeting someone in the grocery line who is a great conversationalist.

> **Delivery zone tip:** *look for signs that you are aligning with your desire, and be grateful for the move in the right direction, even if it is a small step.*

Starting now, you have to realize that the cause of the effect that you are getting in your life is you, your focus, and your feelings. Irrespective of what caused the feeling, it only matters that you control your emotional response to it. To be clear, if you don't stop sending out negative feelings, then you won't stop receiving back negative circumstances.

I have worked with countless clients who came to my office with an understandable reason to be sad, angry, or unhappy. No one is immune from the life events that elicit negative feelings. Many times, after validating the feelings my client was having, I would say – so tell me what's going right? In other words, I was asking them what they have to be grateful for despite the current circumstances. There are biblical references that instruct us to give thanks in all states of being; following this instruction helps us to develop the habit of always looking for the good that exists within our lives.

> Whatsoever things are true, whatsoever things are honest, whatsoever things are just, whatsoever things are pure, whatsoever things are lovely, whatsoever things are of good report; if there be any virtue, and if there be any praise, think on these things (Philippians 4:8 KJV).

There is a protective factor to focusing on good things, not only can it produce goodness in your life, it can also ward off the negative mindset that leads to poor choices and bad habits. Knowing that our thoughts, choices, and habits control the matter that manifests in our lives lends itself to a better understanding of how we can get from where we are now to where we desire to be.

CHAPTER 4

WHERE I WAS

And how I got there

I grew up in a religious yet spiritual household, though it was not without normal challenges. We were a cohesive family with a wholesome and stable living environment, generally centered around church. My father was a praying man who also had many spiritual gifts, one of them being the gift of prophecy. I, being a lot like my dad, naturally saw this gift as desirable and was blessed to accurately give insight about the future to others since the age of three. My father pastored a church, and my mother worked alongside him, and my younger brother and I were active participants in church work. Thankfully, my father always encouraged me to use my own mind and let me know that it was permissible to ask questions, even if it meant asking them of God. At that time, I was less interested in asking God questions than I was asking my parents why people in the church seemed to be so good but often had undesirable life situations. Well, their answers usually left me short of understanding the root cause of this effect. Nonetheless, I always had an inner notion to see and experience God as good and to do as my mother said and treat others the way I wanted to be treated. Fortunately, this kept me in a place of love and happiness most of the time.

Both of my parents experienced physical health challenges that eventually spiraled them into a state of depression, and unbeknownst to me at that time, marital dissatisfaction. I did not become aware of this until I was away at college studying psychology and sociology. I had watched each of my parents take care of the other through various health challenges as well as support each other through the ups and downs of ministry. I knew that they were committed and faithful to each other and shared a marital bond that was consistent with their generation. Most of my parent's friends seemed to have a strong commitment to their marriages, though like my parents, no real guidance on how to joyfully experience life and love.

When I was growing up in the 80s and 90s, media images of healthy relatable Black marriages were virtually non-existent. As an adolescent, I was not frequently exposed to the type of marriage that I thought I wanted when I grew up, in part, because the media images that were available were not consistent with the values of our family. This was reflected in my subconscious programming regarding marriage. The early effects of this seemed minimal, because when I was able to date, the latter part of my high-school years was filled with smart, handsome, fun-loving guys.

Once I was off to college, having been praised for my academic achievement throughout childhood and adolescence, I naturally gravitated toward thoughts and actions that supported my academic work ethic. As a young adult, I set goals consistent with those values and kept my name on the President and Dean's list most of my undergraduate career. This did not leave much time for parties and dating, though there was no lack of invitations. I was labeled as a mature-acting, respectable young woman, and many of the guys

> As a man thinketh in his heart, so is he.
> *Proverb*
> *23:7 KJV*

that asked me out later decided that I was 'wife material,' and they kept me in the friend zone. This started a cycle of me not wanting to be thought of as a wife but as a girlfriend, and it set my internal GPS to later keep me on the path of a single person when what I desired was marriage. In the beginning, I didn't notice this misalignment.

CHAPTER 5

INTENTIONAL THINKING

The key to your getaway car

Nothing in life happens without an intention. Intentions are the catalyst, the fire that powers the entire engine.

So first, you need to have an intention. However, intention setting alone is incomplete for manifesting a new set of circumstances. You need focus, which is sustained attention, to follow it through.

What does this look like in action? You state your desire in the positive present tense and add a feeling word to it.

"I'm so happy that I'm now in a loving relationship."

"I am so grateful that my income has increased by more than $30,000."

"I feel so blessed that our new home is within our budget."

State your desire in the positive, present tense while allowing the feeling of having your desire to encapsulate your being. After doing so, you will need to do a little housekeeping and clear your mind — your environment — eliminating the negative thoughts and reminders that might come up when you say that statement. This will help bring your feelings into alignment with the positive statement you made. It is easier to sustain your focus when your feelings align with your thoughts.

But what if, no matter how hard you try, you can't get rid of the misaligned thoughts and the negative feelings, even though you are saying the positive statement of intention out loud?

Go to the next lowest and more general level that you can actually affirm it and not feel a sense of desperation when you do.

For example, if you say, "I'm so happy I'm in a loving relationship," and you feel despondent every time you say it, that's not the statement for you. You can craft another statement, maybe something like, "I'm so happy that life can lead me into a beautiful relationship."

The next part of this process is to then find somebody that has what you desire and observe them. If you don't know anybody, look outside of your immediate circle. If you want to be in a loving relationship, visit places where families frequent. I made it a point to notice couples every time I was out, and I refused to 'see' anything contrary to my desire. I refused to focus on circumstances that were not aligned with my desire.

CHAPTER 6

STEERING MY THOUGHTS

What you sow will eventually grow

Our decisions are a natural consequence of our focus and imagination. Through our attention, we become like a skilled surgeon changing the very structure of our own brains. Yes, you have that kind of power. The longer you are able to focus on any issue that needs resolution, the more stable the change you make within yourself. Conversely, removing your focus from what you desire before the transformation of your mind takes place weakens the signal you are sending to your desired outcome.

Believe it or not, what you focus on, or see with your mind's eye, is what you get. This concept is wired into your physiology through the reticular activating system (RAS). The RAS is a thumb-sized bundle of neurons located in your brain. Its function is to filter incoming stimuli and assign a level of importance based on what you have decided to focus on. Yes, your brain works to bring things that match your focus to your attention and into your awareness. Have you ever decided to purchase a certain car and then began to notice more of them in your community than before? Well, the neighbors didn't decide to go out and buy that car simply because you like it, they were already there, but your RAS didn't give them a high level of importance because you weren't focused on that brand. This is a highly important aspect of the law of attraction that you shouldn't overlook. You must be especially careful to practice this knowledge during times of challenge and take your focus off any unwanted aspect in your environment. I can personally attest to this truth.

"The only person you are destined to become is the person you decide to be."
Ralph Waldo Emerson

Once I tamed my thoughts enough to get laser-focused on the things that I truly desired, then I began to notice opportunities to form habits that were aligned with my values, and my situation started to change.

T-time – One afternoon, during a telephone conversation with my mother, I stated, "Mother, I didn't realize that I needed to be intentional, or better yet, internally focused on becoming a wife." She replied, "Yeah, you must not have, because anything you put your mind to, you usually accomplish." Still feeling remiss for not realizing this sooner, I said, "Somehow, I thought it would happen just because that's the way life progresses." She then reminded me that life doesn't progress that way for everyone and agreed with me that I should set my intention. I assured her that I would set my intention before the day ended. That was a pivotal point on my journey to becoming a wife. It directed my thoughts to the right path, and with the help of my RAS, my attention soon followed.

It is no secret that as you are searching for peace and prosperity, peace and prosperity are already available to you. As you search for love, love is most assuredly waiting on you. As you search for the right relationships, the right relationships are also looking for you. This can only happen because everything and everyone in this vast Universe is connected.

Let's allow science to help us understand this. Upon microscopic examination of each cell in your fingers, you will find that the DNA in every cell in your hand, is identical to every other cell in the rest of your body. This energy-filled space between each cell in your body is filled with the very essence of the

Creator. This creative power within you connects you to both the Creator and all of creation.

Did you get that part? The very essence of the Creator is woven into the fiber of your being. Everything is energy. The strength of the signal you send out to your desired outcome is powered by the Creative Force behind all things, which is God.

> **Delivery zone tip:** *to reap the benefits of the power living within you, you must plug your thoughts into it.*

Remember, what you focus on, or think about, the most will yield the greatest results in your physical reality. Spiritual leaders and scientist agree that your thoughts influence your outcomes. Both Nicola Tesla and Albert Einstein were proponents of this belief. Intense focus expands the brain and lack of focus causes the neuropathways in that area to diminish. The expansion and contraction of your brain is referred to as neuroplasticity, and it can operate for you or against you. As you imagine your desired outcome, it becomes wired deeper into your mind, therefore, making it a mental fixture. Once the sensory representation, meaning the sight, sound, smell, etc. of your desire is stabilized in your mind, you can then begin to take divinely inspired action to reach your goal. There is no substitute for taking action that is aligned with your vision. You can establish a solid vision for your future by using the focus-forward technique.

> "A man is what he thinks about all day long."
> *Ralph Waldo Emmerson*

CHAPTER 7

FOCUS-FORWARD

Focusing forward to your desired future builds new neural networks that promote positive outcomes and diminish the effect of the current undesirable condition. Never let anyone convince you that your situation is permanent. Your mind shapes your world, and as long as you are able to change your mind, you have the ability to construct your world.

> "We cannot solve our problems with the same level of thinking we used when we created them."
> *Albert Einstein*

Anyone who has ever tried navigating a vehicle while only looking at the road just beyond the hood knows it is impossible to drive this way safely. You must fix your vision further down the road, and in doing so, you can clearly see what is ahead. Guess what? You can also see your destination before you arrive. This is the premise of the focus-forward technique. You can gaze beyond the boundaries of your current state of affairs and see the goodness that awaits you further down the road. Although you may not be able to see your desired destination just yet, you can see yourself on the road that leads to it.

T-time: As a part of her wedding planning, every girl imagines saying "Yes!" to The Dress, and I was no different. I decided to focus-forward to the day that I found the perfect dress. I began by researching the best style of gown for my body type. After that, I characterized the type of bride I wanted to be and cataloged a few pictures that symbolized that to me. After this, I narrowed the selection down to "the one" and placed that picture on my vision board. Seeing that picture reminded me of how happy and relieved I would be once I said "Yes!" to the dress. Keep in mind, I hadn't even said "yes" to a first date with my husband, much less to his proposal, heck, we hadn't even met. That's the advantage of the focus-forward method, you don't have to wait until all the pieces of the puzzle are in place before seeing the finished picture.

Focus, Focus, Focus

Let's take a closer look at how focus functions. Neuroscientists have termed it "selective attention" when your brain filter sifts through and chooses which information to pay attention to, and to impact your future for the better, you must train it to select and hone in on the good you want to see in your life. The two forms of this type of focus are:

1. Hard focus is an intense concentration of intention on a single focal point to the exclusion of all other factors in the environment.
2. Soft focus is a purposeful expansion of awareness to include all aspects of the environment.

Both forms of focus are needed to create our best life. During our quiet time of meditation, we can choose which method of focus our brain is using at that time.

Action step: get a physical picture of your desired destination. Stick it in the lower right corner of a large sheet of paper. Draw a road from the top left corner down to your picture. Place a dot at the half-way point and describe what is there as a sign to let you know that you are on course to reach your destination. See yourself in line to receive the goodness you deserve. Pay attention to your thinking pattern. Choose to place yourself in an infinite loop of positive thinking. Each time you think positively, you move up and get closer to receiving your request. Similarly, each time you have a negative attitude or think a negative thought, you move further from the favorable future you have requested. Before you respond to something or someone in a negative way, ask yourself 1) will this thought get me off course, 2) how will my response affect my progress, and 3) is this worth it?

CHAPTER 8

ENERGY IN MOTION

You are in the driver's seat

Have you ever noticed just how many people you know that complain about the life they are living? It's because most of them have no idea how they get what they have in life. Are they complaining about their growing list of unfulfilled wishes? Or are they complaining about the things they don't want but keep getting? When you hear them, please assure them that it isn't their fault that they've been misguided. They've been told that they are destined for a certain set of circumstances. They, like you, have been taught to focus on what's wrong in their lives and to try to fix it by working harder, taking more action, or networking with others. All of these are necessary, but only after becoming emotionally aligned with what is desired instead of resigning themselves to a luck of the draw attitude. No matter how you look at it, what you feel is what you attract. When you feel happy, your happy vibration solicits more happiness. And, more often than not, those feelings emanate from what you have been focused on.

Many people say they believe feelings have little value. Nothing can be further from the truth. Feelings are not only your communication channel to the Universe, they are also an indicator of how close or far you are from accurately communicating your desire. In other words, feelings are feedback. Feelings are a sensory response to our thoughts and the primary reason that thoughts become things. Let's put it like this, when you transmit positive feelings by thinking positive thoughts, the treasure you receive in return comes from someplace in the palace. However, when you transmit lower level feelings by thinking negative thoughts, what you receive in return comes from someplace in the pit. The moral of the story is to think thoughts that produce high-level feelings. When you find yourself in a place where even thinking a good thought about a particular subject makes you feel bad, then look closer and find a related phrase that makes you feel even slightly better.

Take, for instance, your desire to be happily married. Let's imagine that you have many supportive relationships in your life, so you're doing okay emotionally. But somehow, you know you were meant to enjoy a happy and healthy marital relationship with your spouse. So where is that ideal partner? You've had this desire since you were a young kid playing house with your friends. More than that, you've been thinking about it since your most recent milestone birthday. One day, you open an envelope, and there is an invitation to an old friend's wedding. You pick up the phone and call your closest friend and squawk, "Wow, I don't believe this, guess who is getting married, how did that happen for her and not me? Last I heard, that child was giving her the blues, who would want to marry into that situation?" Envious thoughts start to race through your mind as they churn out negative emotions that course through your body. You failed to remember to rejoice with those who rejoice. So instead of thinking if it happened for her, then surely, there is a way for it to happen for me, you stew in negative emotions. This is precisely why a happy spouse isn't sitting at your dinner table tonight. You have focused on the lack of a spouse in your life rather than the joy of having one. And the only guarantee here is if you continue to send out those feelings of lack about the situation, you are sure to attract more of the same.

Thoughts and feelings have attracting power. Your focus on either positive or negative aspects of your desire will attract more of the same kind of thoughts and feelings regarding the subject. In my counseling practice, I heard this statement from numerous women, "I don't know why I always attract men who cheat." I would learn more by asking them what type of men did you see growing up, what type of men are you friends with now, what T.V. shows do you watch or what type of books do you read? There were usually a variety of sources that consciously or subconsciously told the women that men were cheaters. Not only did I see this in my practice, but I personally knew women who declared that they never wanted to get married. They meant it, too. They cited previous unhappy relationships, disappointment in their fathers or brothers' approach to marriage, statistics, and stories from women they knew as reasons for their decision. Well each of them actually got married and experienced situations that validated their sentiment of not wanting to be married, and for some, the marriage even ended in divorce.

T-time: When I decided to become intentional about being a wife, I focused my attention on sources of information that brought positive images of marriage and relationships into my conscious awareness. I disconnected from cable, mainstream news, and extensive discussions with people about unhealthy relationships of any kind. This helped me to eliminate a constant loop of information that produced thoughts, feelings, and actions that were inconsistent with the image of marriage I intended to create in my life.

What we see and hear conditions us to receive it. You may be saying, I know someone who got married, and she didn't have to do all this changing. Everyone has to become a vibrational match for what they are asking to receive. Although you may not be privy to her inner thoughts and feelings, you have to know that she has focused on being married at some point in time.

Let me give you the formula for changing your focus so you can secure a change in your future – C.A.R.E.

1. **C**haracterize your desire by using one or more of your five senses to define it.
2. **A**ppreciate the goodness that comes along with having your manifested desire. It's also a good idea to be thankful for what you already have in this area.

3. **R**equisition the Universe. Write down the specifications associated with your desire

4. **E**ngage – educate yourself on the details of your desire.

You'll learn more about the CA.R.E. method further on in the book. Back to the issue at hand; the wedding invitation. Now when you attend the wedding you were invited to, you'll be sure to wear a big, sincere smile in celebration of love. And each time after, when you receive the news of a conscious coupling, you will appreciate that someone near to you has found their match. This can be easier said than done but know that the power working within you is able to lead you into thoughts and feelings connected with your greatest and best life.

More T: Shortly after becoming engaged, I hosted a brunch for my bridal entourage. During the brunch, I revealed the wedding color pallet, and the ladies were able to meet and greet each other. The following week, my mother and I had an appointment at a large bridal salon. I decided to allow my inner queen, duchess, and princess to emerge and try on a variety of dresses. They were all beautiful and within my financial reach; however, none of them spoke to me. I decided to narrow my search by setting an appointment at a smaller boutique. The dresses were equally stunning, slightly more expensive, but worth the investment. Still, none were able to satiate my inner bride. You see, many months prior, I had characterized myself as a sophisticated bride. I saw a picture of my dream dress daily and appreciated its beauty and how flattering I believed it would look on me. My request was to easily and effortlessly be guided to my ideal version of that dress. After trying the initial two salons, I focused forward to the happiness I knew I would feel after I located the dress. I engaged by frequently looking for the dress online. One Saturday morning, my fiancé and I went to breakfast with my mother. Afterward, she requested that we go with her to a special occasion boutique because she had a formal event to attend. When we arrived, there was a note to customers saying that the boutique was open on Saturday by appointment only. Being there reminded my mother that she had once gone to a bridal boutique in the vicinity with her good friend for her daughter's dress. At her suggestion, we thought we would take a chance and visit without an appointment. My fiancé dropped us off, and we were greeted with warm smiles and a chilled glass. I tried on several gowns, none of which spoke to me; until I looked in the mirror after getting fitted into one particular dress. I could not resist the happy dance that immediately expressed itself through me. It was brief, but long enough for the bridal consultant to see it and reenact it for my mother while asking her what she thought it meant. By this time, a warmth of happiness flooded my being, and I knew it was the dress of my dreams. Looking back and comparing my dress to the one on my vision board, the similarities are uncanny.

ACTION STEP:

Memorize the C.A.R.E. method.

Do this by learning the first word in each of the four steps above.

Reframe

How many times have you ever framed your picture perfectly on the wall the first time around? Sometimes it takes a little tweaking. Your intentions are like the perfect picture in a frame waiting to be affixed to the wall of your imagination. To reframe your intention, take it out of the negative (I don't want) and bring it around to the positive, present tense (I now have/I Am).

If the only thing you think about is how you don't have it, then guess what? It's going to keep eluding you. This is what you should do instead. Learn to reframe your environment. Make it look as though you have 'it', even when 'it' is not there yet. To do this, you will need to employ your imagination.

This is where you need to be honest with yourself, too. Because if you're saying to yourself, "Well, I don't really know if I want to get married;" if that's the conversation that you tend to have with people to make yourself feel good about not having it, then the Universe responds to that, too. It responds by matching your vibration with someone who does not know if they want to be married, or at least if they do or don't want to be married to you.

If you're ever going to get that change toward the direction that you want to go, you'll need to notice the conversations you have with others and those you have with yourself.

Is your internal dialogue aligned with what you desire to see in your external environment?

Internal dialogue is the inner chatter that's constantly going on inside our heads.

It is a distraction when we give our attention to that small, critical voice in our own head that says, "No, you cannot have what you desire."

"No, I don't think that you are smart enough to be successful."

"You aren't good enough to be happy."

Our inner dialogue is usually guided by our inner critic that tells us, "No" to everything we desire and gives a long list of supporting reasons.

"If you don't like something, change it. If you can't change it, change your attitude."
Maya Angelou

If we continue to listen to our inner critic and allow it to guide our every move, then it's no wonder that we aren't living our best life, because this inner critic has got us focusing on the wrong things. We have to begin the process of reversing our internal programming to foster alignment with what we desire to see in the external world. Prayer and meditation are excellent tools to bring a sense of calm to the mind and clear the mental canvas for a new picture.

ACTION STEP:

The ID Badge

Your inner dialogue is like an ID badge. The things you say to yourself day after day is your identity, your ID badge. Take a day to listen to your inner dialogue and see what kind of ID badge you are making for yourself. Which ID badge did you wake up with today?

What ID badge do you desire to wake up with tomorrow morning?

Take a selfie. Send yourself a text using the selfie. Type five one word descriptions about your best self for your new ID badge.

Meditation

Meditation calms our world from the inside out and is one way to create positive life experiences, raise your creative vibration, and move yourself into a place to expect that which you have asked to receive. Meditation, mindfulness, and thoughtfulness demand sustained focus of the mind. By meditating, you silence the thoughts that are on autopilot. You completely shut them down, and you say, "I have elevated my mind to a state of quiet." Many people mistakenly believe that having a lot on their mind is a symbol of productivity; however, less is more.

In the process of true meditation, you have fewer thoughts, and the fewer thoughts that you have competing for your attention, the more you're able to have a clean slate to ask for what you desire, without all those depressing or anxiety producing thoughts blocking it, clamoring to be heard. Instead, you choose what to focus on, rather than focusing on those thoughts that are running rampant at any given time.

Meditation is a process that naturally brings you into a neutral state. Similarly, when we engage in prayer, our minds are quieted, and our thoughts are directed. With meditation, as with affirmation, it is best to identify where you are on your journey and start there.

> **ACTION STEP:**
>
> Research various forms of meditation and implement one for the next 5 days.

Using Prayer

Prayer in its many forms is a powerful tool when used to connect with the desires of your heart. Prayer teaches you how to go in the opposite direction of the negative inner chatter. It allows your inner self to take the lead and direct the course of the conversation that you have with God and with yourself. When you pray, you are communing with the power that created the world from nothingness. Prayer is a way of being that helps us continually sift through our inner thoughts to keep what is useful and disengage from what is not.

Prayers of Supplication mean you are asking for something, and Prayers of Thanksgiving is being thankful for what you have, and for also knowing that what you ask for is available to you, now. After your prayers are said and done, you then have to allow your answered prayers to emerge into your reality.

Prayers of Supplication and Prayers of Thanksgiving run parallel to steps 2 and 3, appreciation and requisition, of the C.A.R.E. process. I encourage you to use prayer as often as needed. The practice of meditation and prayer is person dependent, and there is no one right way to approach it. There is no pressure for you to have an all-night shut-in every weekend. Simply find one short sentence that you pray each time that you think about your desire throughout the day when you are in the appreciation and requisition phases of your journey. This will help safeguard your desire from distractions.

CHAPTER 9

DISTRACTIONS

The fork in the road

If someone is always talking to you about how tough life is, how terrible things are, and you decide to echo their sentiments and say, "Yeah, I know. The same thing happened to me, only worse." You're participating in this person's pessimism, and by doing that, you are allowing their will to influence your own environment. You're allowing them to direct your focus. It's time to learn how to direct your own focus so you can achieve your dreams.

But before we do that, let's explore this a little further.

The advent of the text message and other limited character messaging has weakened our attention span. So much so, that it's what we expect now when communicating on our devices. If a message or social media post is longer than short, we just keep scrolling. If what we desire doesn't come quickly, we also give up and think that it just wasn't meant to be. When the reality is we haven't trained our brain to faithfully focus on our desire long enough to actually bring it into our reality. We are in a loop, listening to our internal dialog, which is how we got to where we are, and focusing on the wrong thing, which is why we want to be somewhere else. But if you can't focus on it, then you can't construct it and call it into your future.

Overall, we have access to vast amounts of media, which has led to overconsumption of information in the opposite direction of our desire.

T-time: As I approached my late 20s and early 30s, there was no shortage of songs that praised the independent woman. I certainly didn't need a song to tell me to be what I already was, but the momentum of the movement kept me inspired to be all that I could be, independently. As I found myself surrounded by like-minded women who were i.n.d.e.p.e.n.d.e.n.t., I finally realized what that meant in my circle of friends. We were all bringing home the dough, baking it, enjoying eating it, and sharing recipes with each other, not our husbands. I was a clinical director of an agency, running my own private practice, and at that time, studying for a doctorate in psychology. In many ways, building my independence was keeping me distracted from the relationship that I desired to have. I wasn't taking the time to create a realistic picture of an ideal marriage for me. I was running on past programming. I had seen the women in my family raise a family while supporting the men in their lives by working along with them in ministry and taking little thought of what they wanted for themselves. I began to wonder if I had what it took to have a happy and successful marriage, and somewhere along the way, I became fearful that I would fail at it (internal GPS set). Not realizing that fearing that I may not get it right was a download into my internal navigation system or my subconscious mind, I continued to move along on the path that had been unconsciously set to girlfriend.

My long-term, committed relationships were with men of exquisite taste, so there was always something to look forward to on the dating scene. My enjoyment of these dates sent signals to the Universe to keep sending me more of them.

I loved dating, the fun-times from high-school dating coupled with being treated so delicately by the guys I went out with during my college years left me with great anticipation of full-grown adult dating. Unbeknownst to me, it appeared that dating was my set point, my comfort zone; this mindset stemmed from vows, commitments, and standards that I had set for myself in my early teens that made it simpler for me to not get too serious unless I was married. Nonetheless, as an adult, I liked having plans, getting dolled up, and anticipating the highlights of the date, and yes, looking forward to the next one. However, this grew old as I approached my early-30s, as I watched others get married and start families. Not to mention the quality of the men I began to attract seemed to be on a downward spiral that I had no clue how to stop.

Thankfully, this was around the time that the self-help community was inundated with books on finding "Mr. Right." I found one book on the subject that spoke to me, and just to get the most out of the money I spent on it, I decided to follow one of the many exercises from its pages. It was simply making a list of the qualities I wanted in a partner. Over the course of a few nights, I had listed 100 qualities. The Universe responded, and before I knew it, I had met a handful of men, each with 4 or 5 of the 100 characteristics qualities I had written down. Not exactly the results I was hoping for, but I could see some of the pieces starting to add up. A few years had passed and still no lasting love. By then, many of my friends and family who had gotten married were starting to get divorced, or at least verbalizing their unhappiness, which compounded my fear of failure in marriage and had me thinking if they couldn't do it, then what were the chances that I could. And did I mention that my parent's marriage of 42 years looked to be nearing its last heartbeat as well?

In my early 30s, I, with my independent self, had decided to build a house, and while moving in and unpacking boxes, I found a journal, it was unused. However, when I opened it, there were two sheets of paper folded between the pages. I smiled as I remembered back to the nights a few years prior that I wrote the 100 physical, spiritual, and other qualities that I wanted in a partner. This re-ignited my commitment to be in a relationship. I revisited that list and narrowed it down to a more manageable size. I reviewed it a few times over the course of a month, but soon returned to the norm of focusing on helping others. A few months after this, I learned that one of my favorite researchers on the brain and child development was the keynote speaker at a conference, and I decided to go. It happened to be in a town near a good friend, and she asked me if I wanted to go out for dinner and music. I said yes, and she sent me the venue address. Little did I know that the list of 100 qualities would materialize into my life that evening. Well it did, and over the next few months, I was increasingly shocked that one person could be a large percentage of the very unrealistic list that I had written out. Time went on, and each date seemed to be better than the last, and each moment brought us closer to each other and our happily ever after. But wait, I still hadn't reprogrammed my internal GPS from girlfriend to wife.

Let's look at this a little more closely by showing you an example.

If you think about the person who wants to get married, it can be one of the more challenging things to just think about being married because you tend to feel even more alone when you do. Thinking about being married or going on a date while feeling alone creates dissonance between you and your desire. When your thoughts about your desire are disharmonious with your feeling about your desire the Universe responds to your feelings.

This is why it is imperative that you give focused attention to what it is you desire to see better in your life. So even if you have feelings of hurt and disappointment, deal with them but don't ruminate on them. Ruminating on them only makes you a magnet for more of what you've been getting, that you don't want. It's a self-perpetuating situation. It's your ID badge. If you're giving your attention to being alone, "Here's your ID badge. Alone!"

It is more productive to focus, instead, on the feelings that will bring you closer to your desires.

ACTION STEP:

Now that you're aware of distractions, it's time to identify what it is you actually desire to be, then look at what's distracting you or what's holding your attention, and ask yourself the question, "Does this serve my desire or is this a distraction?"

CHAPTER 10

RECLAIMING MY ATTENTION

Building a bridge to somewhere

You must construct a mental picture to bridge the gap between internal focus and external reality.

Sticking with the example from the previous chapter of 'alone' versus 'being in a relationship'...

When you decide that you don't want to be alone, you have to get a picture of yourself not being alone. You have to get a picture of yourself in a community, in a relationship, and you have to change your "ID badge."

You have to say to yourself, "You know, I'm a really great conversationalist," or, "Wow, I'm a really wonderful supporter," or, "I'm a really great cheerleader." And those are things that help you learn to be communal or in relationship with others. So when you decide you're going to have a spouse, you can say (and believe), "Oh, I know that I'm really great at cheerleading people on," and, "He wants to start a business, so yeah, this could actually work."

A lot of times, it's hard for us to see the big picture when we have been so long without our desire, especially when it comes to relationships. So you need to get a mental picture of yourself with the thing, or a relationship you desire to have, so your mindset can change. Seeing yourself with something you've never had is hard. I suggest starting with a mental picture first, but if you cannot conjure up a mental picture, start with something easier, like, 'What's the house going to sound like?' 'What's it going to smell like when there's someone else in the house, and you are cooking more?' Or 'What are you going to hear?' 'What music are you going to listen to that's different than what you listen to now?'

If your answer is nothing, then everything will stay the same for you. You're not ready to embrace a new awareness.

You have to engage the multifaceted dimensions of the object or relationship that you want to bring into your life. You can find a way to create a picture with sound as opposed to with just visual images. Furthermore, you won't have to walk around with your vision board in your back pocket; although I'm certain there is a phone app for that if you want to. The point is that you would burn out if you tried to visualize all day every day. If you only dream and dream and dream, your well of creative inspiration will quickly short circuit, your dreams would appear even more deferred, and your focus would fade. You would soon be back to the drawing board and looking for new ways to renew your vision. Sometimes you will need to have a vision, but also hear the sounds associated with your big picture or feel the textures in the environment of your dream come true.

There are times when you learn visually, times when things make more sense auditorily, and other times, when kinesthetics is the most viable option for getting the point. Let's face it, life is not one dimensional, and neither can our engagement with it be; we've got to infuse our expectations with all of the sights, sounds, and smells that we can fit into the construction story, so that you can seamlessly evolve into the   (fill in the blank)   that you desire to be.

The next phase involves addressing your beliefs.

Limiting Beliefs

A limiting belief is an inaccurate thought that feels like a fact, and you address it by questioning its origin, its validity, and its stability. You overcome limiting beliefs with persistence and steady progress in the direction of your intended outcome.

Do you really believe what you desire is possible, even though you heard a statistic that a large percentage of people like you never get it?

Do you believe that it's possible for you, do you believe that you can be in the group that does?

Do you believe you have what it takes to receive all that you desire?

And if you don't?

Begin to go through the process of asking yourself questions as to why you believe the things you believe around what you desire. And no matter what the answer is to that question, start to reprogram yourself to believe that it is possible for you by seeing that other people actually have it — by reading and even writing stories about the people that do.

Create the mental picture of your desire.

> "First, I dream my painting, and then I paint my dream."
> *Vincent Van Gogh*

Consciously bringing it into your mental or your physical environment is crucial. By seeing other people with it, other people like you with it, and noticing those people more helps your subconscious mind to say, "Hmm…I can relax that dis-belief a little bit."

It's about changing your mindset to take you in the right direction. Your mindset determines the results you get in your life.

ACTION STEP:

Start affirming that what you desire is good. You also have to look at why you don't believe that what you desire is possible for you. Examine other limiting beliefs that may be there, too.

Construction Zones

The brain, previously viewed as unable to change and diminishing with age, is now scientifically proven to be adaptable and malleable. In fact, the physical structure of your brain changes as you think, which means it changes all of the time.

Each morning, you awaken with new nerve cells that are there to assist you in constructing a healthy mental environment. The Creator so graciously gives us the opportunity to awaken to renewed possibilities each day.

You can unwire negative patterns by consciously directing your thinking in a positive direction; new thought networks emerge as you do this. This is called neurogenesis, and it is why you can wake up every morning excited to create your day. The brain is the instrument of the mind, and our mind is designed to control the body. Paying attention via the function of thinking activates the inner atmosphere of your physical body.

In simpler terms, you are a walking, biological, response system to everything that's in your environment. For every thought that you have, there is a chemical reaction that happens inside of you. There is a chemical response to every thought that you think, and the accumulation of those responses change the receptor site on your neurotransmitters. They are programmed to start the chain reaction in your body that makes you have more corresponding thoughts. Whenever we have feelings of any kind, each individual emotion releases its very own set of neuropeptides. And those neuropeptides begin to course through the body. Then they link up with the receptors, which in turn, change the structure of the cell.

We are programmed at a cellular level to respond to our own thoughts. Not just other people's; that does affect you as well, but you are biologically encoded with a tendency to respond to your own thoughts first and foremost.

The good news is that this can change; your body goes through a process of regeneration regularly.

Without getting too deeply into the science of this, we can see how magnificent and intricately woven our physical, mental, and emotional bodies are, and that one has an effect on the other. We know now that your mental perception sets the tone and has a great effect on your physical well-being as well as the reality that you see in your life on a daily basis. All of these chemical reactions in your body, whether they are positive or negative, you have some control over changing them.

Every time you have a thought, you start a neurochemical reaction. Thoughts produce words and behaviors that create a feeling inside us. Once we have a feeling, we tend to think more thoughts associated with it, which leads to a potentially endless cycle of that feeling.

Fortunately, we have a choice about where we pay attention and can immediately change our focus to create thoughts associated with a better feeling future.

You get to choose how you focus your attention.

Paying attention, like learning a new language, is a skill that can be improved upon with practice.

Now that you have become aware that there's a biological response to the thoughts that you think and the words that you say, let's continue to watch our words and monitor our thoughts.

CHAPTER 11

SHIELD OF INTENTION

Live life by design, not by default

Keep in mind that people who accomplish extraordinary goals, or who are successful, are exactly the same as you, except they set and focus on their goals and take inspired action to achieve them. They are not immune to distractions, but the power of their intention is so strong that it forms a protective layer that allows inspired action to flow in and flush out unfruitful attempts to manifest their desire.

> "Always stay true to yourself and never let what somebody says distract you from your goals."
> *Michelle Obama*

Before deciding to write this book, I was so drawn to the subject of intention that I created a weekly podcast and a website appropriately coined *"intentionaire."* In my research for those projects, I confirmed that everything ever made or achieved began with an intention, and I reaffirmed beyond any doubt that we are the heirs of our intention. There is a consensus among researchers, scholars, and teachers on the definition of intention as a purpose or aim to accomplish a desired outcome. Intentionaires, as I like to call people who live intentionally, power their intention with a strong determination. These people have a resolve about themselves that won't allow anyone or anything to run interference on or intercept the manifestation of their dreams. Are you one of those people who form an internal picture of your desire and tirelessly runs to the finish line with it?

T-time: I see myself as a highly intentional being. Without the power of intention, I could not have graduated on time with my doctorate degree. You see, my research chair went on sabbatical from the university the same semester that I was scheduled to complete my research and graduate. To complicate things, I hadn't gotten IRB (Institutional Review Board) approval for the study of human subjects that was required for this phase of my research study. How could the faculty chair of my research leave me in that position? And to further compound the situation, the IRB process was back-

logged for more than 6 months after a change in administration at the university. Each time I called the office to request an appeal (as my graduation date approached), I was told that there were a few hundred other scientific proposals ahead of mine, and there was no way that my project could go through the appeal process, much less obtain approval before April. Well, I was already on the calendar to defend my research in April. It looked impossible, but I had to remain focused. I could not give up. I contacted the office daily, often multiple times; I followed every lead offered to me by my fellow classmates and other experienced scientists, still no progress.

Anxiety crept in, and soon, minor stomach pains had grown into stifling bouts of endo duodenal problems that prohibited me from even thinking about food most days much less eating it without severe repercussions. I confided in two good friends who were also in the upcoming graduating class. They encouraged me and assured me that I would graduate on time with my class. After watching the weeks, days, hours, minutes, and seconds of my unapproved study of human subjects application sit in a queue awaiting approval, I knew that the odds were insurmountable. I tried to think of a way to allow my mind to accept that completing my research and graduating at a later time was inevitable, and most importantly, insignificant. Out of nowhere, I received a text message from my brother who I had not told of my dilemma. It said, "It's already done" and included a link to a song that completely uplifted my outlook and reenergized my resolve to obtain approval, analyze the data, and complete the study on schedule. After setting a strong intention, writing my name on a sticky note with my new doctoral level credentials, and posting it where I could see it, I picked up the phone to contact the university and insisted on a solution that would lead me to graduate with my class. What happened next was unbelievable. The young lady who answered the phone and took messages from students who were requesting an appeal accused me of having already completed my research without board approval. Wait…what? Any social scientist knows that it is unethical and potentially unlawful to do such a thing. Be mindful that the project had already received board approval from the medical university; I simply had not obtained approval from my university to conduct my specific study. Although the data was waiting for me to unlock it, I had taken every precaution to not handle it, even after being informed that I had approval through the medical school. I was taking no chances, and yet, after being so careful, this was actually happening to me. The following evening, I opened my school email account and found an email from the director of the doctoral program advising me that I had to attend a meeting before the Board of Regents regarding a report that I had already conducted and written my study. I immediately popped in my ear-buds and listened to the song my brother had sent me for the remaining waking hours while envisioning myself in a cap and gown amongst my classmates and writing my name with my new doctorate level credentials on my personalized stationery, yes, I did this for hours. The next day came, and I had to contend with my normal environment of dealing with coworkers and seeing patients, all the while, moving along as though everything was sunshine and rainbows, but feeling as if I were standing under a cloud in the rain. Well, the day of my conference with the Board of Reagents was upon me, and all I could do was be honest and pray that my integrity and commitment to improving the mental health of patients affected by my research would come through. After asking a few questions and reading my written statement, the board unanimously decided that I had not violated any part of the scientific process, and that I did have clearance to review the data (although I hadn't looked at it) since the study was indeed approved by the medical university and I was a co-investigator on the project. Vindication! A testament to the power of faithful focus.

My intention to conduct my research had prevailed, and little did I know, the Universe had conspired to assist me in a way that I never could have imagined would result from such a challenge. One member of the board of regents interjected, "It looks like your IRB application has been caught in the approval bottleneck." And before I could respond, he said there are enough board members here to approve your application right now. Since they had already read my application in preparation for the board review, they again unanimously motioned to approve my application; therefore, allowing me the opportunity to move forward with my research. Vindication and Victory! At the beginning of the conference when I had asked what reason the young lady gave for this review, the primary reason she gave was that I was so confident that I could complete the study and graduate with my class that she suspected that I had already completed it, because otherwise, it would be impossible to do. I cannot tell you all the events thereafter that arranged themselves perfectly to allow me to complete and defend my research, albeit at the last second of the last hour on the last remaining day.

Since that defining moment, the unseen power of intention has been as apparent to me as the breath I breathe. I hope that this will help you to view intention with a new set of eyes and to see intention setting as an invisible form of insurance on your future plans.

Goal clarity is your gateway to success. Placing your goals on paper is one of the most important first steps you can take to physically anchor your desired intention into the annals of your mind.

Ask yourself – What is my desire? How do I take my first step toward manifesting this desire? Which specific action must I take to begin? When shall I begin? I trust that your answer to the last question is "now."

If so, use the following page to jot down your ultimate goal in the identified domain.

Co-Creative Consciousness – your divinity, your creative ability

_____

_____

Assets – wealth, money, bank account, paycheck, property, investments

_____

_____

Relationships – personal, professional, romantic, relatives, coworkers, colleagues, friends, siblings, parents

_____

_____

Empowerment – mental health, physical health, social well-being, self-esteem

_____

_____

Consider each domain and select one to focus on as you continue to read.

_____

_____

Take Action: Draw a shield.

Shield[3]
/SHēld/

noun

- a broad piece of metal or another suitable material, held by straps or a handle attached on one side, used as a protection against blows.
- One that protects or defends.
- A decorative or identifying emblem.

Verb

- protect (someone or something) from a danger, risk, or unpleasant experience.

Earlier in the book, I told you that the C.A.R.E. method integrates a heart-mind approach to manifestation, which is what makes it so powerful. When using the shield of intention, you must characterize or give definition to your desire in each domain with both words and pictures. You need to get the picture of your present desire for your life in that domain and then use words to further describe and define that desire. Doing this ensures that you utilize both the left and right hemispheres of your brain. The left side is the logical thinking side, and the right side is the feeling side, and both are absolutely necessary for the process of manifesting our intentions. Many times, when we are thinking about our desires, we do one of two things. We think without feeling, or we have a lot of feelings, usually negative ones, but we do not have a definition to give to it. So to bring this point home, let's examine a passage from the one book that has been purchased or referenced more than any other book on earth, the Bible.

Let's refer to the words of *The* Christ in Matthew 6:7 (KJV) – "But when ye pray, use not vain repetitions, as the heathen do: for they think that they shall be heard for their much speaking…" Now when you are in a group and there is one particular person who is talking more than anyone else in the room, what is the first thing you do? Someone probably says you tune them out – well, you cannot tune them out until after you hear them, right? But in this passage, we are told that the one who speaks much will not be heard. In the phrase, use not vain repetitions, the definition of the word vain[4] is "producing no result, useless." Ask yourself, why did The Master Teacher say using a lot of words was fruitless in our efforts to be heard by the Most High? It is because words are actually a human communication tool. People have been communicating with each other since the beginning of time. Language, however, may not have been developed until as recent as 50,000 years ago.

If the human vocabulary has only been online for such a short period of time, how did people initially communicate with each other? I don't have a definitive answer for you on this; however, I can say it was likely with their expressed and possibly even their unexpressed feelings. Words symbolize the human idea of the thing that is desired. However, symbols are used to evoke a feeling. Why do you think companies have a logo? A logo is a symbol that a company uses to evoke a feeling in you when you see it. And in the same way that companies communicate with us, we must learn to communicate in harmony with the Divine Mind.

As you know, a single word can have such varied meanings and be so heavily used that it loses its potency in our minds. This is why a picture can be worth a thousand words. Painting a picture in your mind helps you to bypass the brain's logic and move right over to the creative center. The right hemisphere of your brain is the creative center of your being and the initial place you go thru to communicate with the Creator. Feeling is the communication tool of the right hemisphere.

Words have regional meanings. Feelings, on the other hand, are universal. In fact, feelings are your most valuable communication tool. When you see a picture of someone expressing an emotion, you don't necessarily have to see a word associated with the feeling before your mirror neurons allow you to empathize with it.

Let's go again to the Good Book for some insight on this and look at Psalm 9:1 (KJV) which says – "I will give thanks to you, Lord, with all my heart; I will show forth all thy marvelous works." Notice it does not say with all my mouth, with all my words, or with all my phrases), it says with all my heart – the heart is the feeling processing center of your being. Note the semicolon, which signifies the start of a new but related thought in the same sentence. The verse later goes on to say – I will tell of all your wonderful deeds. The word 'tell' naturally connotes a verbalization or the use of words; notice that this is after communicating with feeling first.

Linking this together and tying it into the shield of intention, you must approach each domain of the shield as a visual representation of the good you are ready to receive in that domain of your life. You will need one image and one affirmation. After which, you should infuse your symbol with the feeling of the word you have chosen. You do this by making the definition of that word personal and meaningful.

> **Delivery zone tip:** *Begin with the end in mind. Planning for an arrival to your destination takes effort. If all of this is sounding like it may take more than a moment, you are correct; however, it does not have to take an entire lifetime for you to experience the joy of consciously manifesting your desire in your life.*

The next part of weaving this all together is to craft a powerful 'I AM' statement for each domain and use it with the Shield of Intention.

The 'I Am' statements are simply another tool to help you faithfully focus on the now. Because whatever you declare yourself to be, "I am…," you're saying, "I am, like, 'this' now." Whether you are that or not does not matter. Your brain doesn't know the difference, but if you consistently say, 'I Am,' then that you must become.

These are some 'I AM' statements that I wrote for the shield of intention. They are general guidelines that should be consistent with your values, you can get even more specific when you select a domain.

#1 Co-Creative Consciousness

I Am a Co-creative Conscious being, an authentic reflection of the love, light, and power of the Divine Mind.

#2 Assets –

I Am a Prosperous Being. Full of the power to get wealth, to maintain multiple streams of income, and to grow in good financial success.

#3 Relationship –

I Am a Relational Being – filled with the joy of right connections with individuals, organizations, and communities that contribute to my personal and professional advancement.

#4 Empowerment –

I Am a well being – filled with an abundance of health and wholeness in every area of my mind, body, and spirit.

When you need some inspiration, repeat your 'I AM' statement. Focusing on who you have declared yourself to be will help you push past internal resistances to fully embrace your transformation.

Shields are treasured armor. "He took away the treasures of the house of the LORD and the treasures of the king's house, and he took everything, even taking all the shields of gold which Solomon had made." I Kings 14:26

Shields are strength. "He put shields and spears in every city and strengthened them greatly." 2 Chronicles 11:12.

Shields are used to communicate safety. "After these things the word of the LORD came to Abram in a vision saying, 'do not fear Abram, I am a shield to you, your reward shall be very great'." Genesis 15:1

Shields are used to communicate promotion. "But you O LORD are a shield about me, My glory, and the One who lifts my head." Psalm 3:3 You have also given me the shield of your salvation and your help makes me great." Psalm 18:35

Shields are a refuge. "You are my hiding place and my shield; I wait for your word." Psalm 119:115

Shields are a help. "Our soul waits for the LORD; He is our help and our shield." Psalm 33:22

Shields carry rewards. "For the Lord God is a sun and shield: the Lord will give grace and glory: no good thing will he withhold from them that walk uprightly." Psalm 84:11

Your shield is your point of reference if you lose your way. Use it as a frame for creating a visual story of where you desire to go.

CHAPTER 12

C.A.R.E.

Your roadmap from here to there

As we go further into the C.A.R.E framework, we need to make sure you're clear on where it is you desire to go.

What is it that you desire to have more of or bring into your physical awareness?

When was the last time you assessed your values? Not the values that were handed down to you from your parents or consciously and subconsciously ingrained in you from your environment.

The values that I'm speaking of are written upon the tablet of your heart. These values speak to you from within and serve as a guidepost for your happiness in each of the four domains.

Your values and intentions should be consistent with your internal picture of your best life. Think back to a time in your life when your actions were aligned with your values or your truest desire for yourself. What was the outcome?

value[5]

ˈvalyoo':/

noun

1. principles or standards of behavior; one's judgment of what is important in life.

Acknowledging your values is vital to ensuring that you are in sync with them.

Start by doing a little soul searching as to what you value.

Next, look in a dictionary for the definition of the thing you value.

What goals have you set in accordance with your values? Write one sentence for each domain.

What action steps are needed to accomplish your goals? Identify one action word to associate with each domain.

What images can you find that support your inner vision? Select one image for each domain and place it on the shield.

Make sure your desired destination is aligned with your personal values. Like a car that is in need of an alignment, you are likely to veer off course if you are headed toward a destination to which you are not connected. For instance, if you value and enjoy relaxing vacation destinations with sunshine and tropical breezes you would be misaligned with your value if you set out to climb a snow-capped mountain for your next getaway.

Characterize your desire – *be definite with the infinite*

I echo the sentiments of Rev. Dr. Johnnie Coleman and others who say to be definite with the infinite. The Universe is infinite in supply, and to pull something out of the Universal storehouse, you need to be very specific about what you desire to receive. When I say, 'Be definite with the Infinite,' I mean there is no end to what God is or can be, God is infinite. Consider a large piece of fabric. How do you create an outfit? You decide what you want to wear, and then you cut it out using a pattern. God is the fabric of all creation. And to get anything from God, you have to carve out that specific thing, in the atmosphere, in time, in your awareness.

That is how you become definite with the Infinite. You characterize your desire. You give it character, an ID badge, a name, an adjective, a description. You create the picture of it, you create the thought of it, you create the sound of it. You become the creative director of your very own internal program.

Creation starts with an idea of what you desire and moves you toward an inner knowing. This framework takes your desire from abstract to specific. In fact, desire activates this part of the process. Your desire lights the fire within you that gets you focused and helps you to create the intention to which you need to give your attention.

The same is true with characterizing your desire. If you can't define your desire, then you are not paying enough attention to it. You can only write down the details of your desire if you pay attention to that specific desire.

The attention process is woven throughout the entire C.A.R.E. framework.

We're all still in search of something, whether that's more abundance or more harmony with loved ones. Many of my values were apparent in my life;

however, my desire to express my affinity for marriage seemed afar. The moment I characterized the type of marriage that felt realistic for me, my definition then aligned with my values in a way that assured me that what I desired was within my reach. I then characterized the physical, spiritual, financial, and other qualities of my ideal partner.

Early in the process, I physically characterized the man of my dreams as one with a bald head and a thick, neat beard. I don't ever recall these physical qualities as being my "type" in the past, but it was a growing trend among men that happened to catch my eye. Whenever I noticed that specific look in a magazine, or even in person, I would pause to appreciate it. After meeting my husband, I complimented him on his nice clean-shaven head and his very thick, neat, black beard. His response surprised me. He stated that about two weeks prior to meeting me he felt he needed a change and decided to shave his thinning hair off completely and grow out his beard. He's so handsome.

If you're not sure how to characterize what you desire, start by defining your values.

Answer these questions:

- What is important to you?
- What makes you happy?
- What are you passionate about?
- What inspires you?

Appreciate – *What you appreciate adds value to your intention*

When you want to create something you don't have, look around at what you do have that is similar, and then lavish the Universe with thanksgiving for something you already have in that domain. This gets your energy flowing in the right direction.

For example, if you desire better health, choose the Empowerment Domain. Using one or more of your five senses imagine one area of your body returning to optimal health. Think about what it means to you to have better health, and then begin to appreciate your current and future health status.

Doing this raises your vibration, which allows you to get into the flow of your desire; thereby, exponentially magnifying your ability to connect with it.

Have you ever complimented your friend on something they were wearing? What does that lead you to do? Focus on it, right?

It leads you to pay attention to it, to the color of it, the texture, etc. And often, one compliment leads to another.

You have to be focused on something to appreciate it.

When you appreciate something, you are giving your full attention to it. And that's what the creative process requires, faithful focus.

Appreciation is a universal currency. It is accepted everywhere and works well to keep you faithfully focused on the manifestation of your desire. Please understand that this is not a suggestion that you should charm your desire into reality. Your appreciation needs to be genuine and authentic. Appreciation is the fuel that keeps your engine running while you wait for your manifestation.

Appreciation is akin to praise except it is more values-driven. Praise is general. Appreciation is specific. Appreciation necessitates both context and content. Making it more meaningful than praise alone and it sends the angels and all of heaven moving in your direction.

Think about this: who wants to be in the presence of someone that doesn't appreciate them? No one. So if you are asking for more money and you don't appreciate money, you are going to find a way to spend it without it accomplishing your goal.

This is also true for your desires; they don't naturally show up in an atmosphere that is hostile toward them. By being appreciative for the desire that is on its way, you are paving a path for it to smoothly land right in your delivery zone.

> **Delivery zone tip:** *knowing the aspects of your desire for which you are most appreciative helps you to requisition with greater accuracy.*

There is a particular couple that I admire for their seamless relationships with their in-laws. Both sides of their families vacation together, and the in-law title does not exist between them. I admire the ease with which their families blend, and I verbalized my appreciation to them for being a shining example. On my first vacation with my husband, I met his brother and his brother's wife, she and I happened to share the same profession and connected over that common bond. Because I had previously tuned my attention into effortless relationships, getting to know them felt genuine and easy.

As an added bonus, when we were dating, the first time my husband met anyone in my family, which happened to be my aunt and uncle, they each, at a separate time and without hearing the other, told him they felt like they knew him from somewhere. Soon thereafter, we arrived at another relative's birthday event, and one of my favorite cousins was walking away from the building as we were walking toward it. Upon approaching us, he hugged my now husband and was like, hey man, I haven't seen you in a long time (my husband looks nothing like any of my previous partners). When I told him they had never met, he said he looked so familiar that he thought he knew him. This magic repeated itself at least 12 more times that very night, and that is no exaggeration. Many of my male cousins and my uncles thought they knew him. This increased my confidence that this could become a lifelong relationship because I had previously desired and admired this very thing.

The intensity of my desire, admiration, requisition, and engagement with this was so strong that it continued even after we married. Almost two years later, when attending a family event on my father's side of the family, there was more man-bonding magic in the air. My two cousins who were fraternity brothers with my husband, although they had never met, greeted my husband in the driveway upon his arrival, and they were talking, laughing, and sharing such great comradery that I thought they had somehow met, and I forgot about it. When I went over to greet my husband and tell him I must have forgotten that he had met my cousins, they all looked at me and said, this is our first-time meeting. All I could do was smile at knowing that what you appreciate returns to add value to your life.

ACTION STEP:

Find an object that you appreciate and write down all the things about that object that you appreciate. If it's a physical, tangible object that you are holding in your hand, notice the weight of it, notice the texture of it — you automatically become attuned to the thing that you are appreciating. While doing this, notice that you have to faithfully focus on it to appreciate it.

Requisition — *know your request*

T-time: After I found those journals with the 100 characteristics while moving into my new home, I thought I needed a way to rekindle my connection with what I was asking for in a romantic partner. Although, at that time, I had not coined the focus-forward technique, that is exactly what I did. I made an outline of some of the things that I would do with Mr. 100, once I met him, that signified that we were in a serious, committed relationship with potential for marriage. At the time, I was simply doing this to let myself know what stage I considered the relationship to be in when we reached certain milestones. Well, I decided to focus on the "we just got serious" phase, and I outlined our first vacation together. Most people of my generation would say it's pretty serious if a couple travels together. So I decided where I wanted to go. It was a place that I had actually visited in childhood. I looked up the tourist guide for that state and wrote down a few of the attractions. I vividly remember seeing the pictures and appreciating the beauty of the town. To make what could be a long story short, after meeting Mr. 100 and going on a few dates, he asked me what was something that I would like to do more. Now this was an aside as he was walking me to my car after our date. I told him that I would like to travel more. Having spent so much time in school and building a career afterward, I hadn't made much time for adventure. I had also secretly declared that I was not going on any more girls' trips, although they were always filled with the stomach-burning laughter that signifies a good time, until after I was romantically coupled. He asked me where I wanted to go, and I immediately told him the city that I had written in my notebook months before I met him. Ironically, he had previously lived there and had been saying to himself that he needed to return for a visit.

> **Delivery zone tip:** *what you are looking for is also looking for you.*

Request - Make your request known.

This part of the C.A.R.E. method mandates that you identify what you desire and then put in your request for it. It's also the part of the framework that people struggle with the most.

You would be surprised how many people feel as though they need permission to desire something good for themselves.

With most clients, when we get to the requisition part of the C.A.R.E process, they say, "You don't know how hard this is for me." I usually respond with, "But this is what you say you desire."

Too which they reply, "It is, but it's hard for me to ask for it. I don't know how to do that."

Sound familiar?

I offer creative ways to hold my clients accountable to their dreams and support them in shifting their mindsets to get unstuck, but the fact of the matter is the requisition part of the process is where most people are the least prepared.

Although we feel entitled to many things, we often feel entitled in the context of what someone else has or is doing. We want it because we think someone else does not deserve it, and we should have it instead. In our personal lives, we are timid about feeling entitled to goodness.

You might think that another person is more special than you, or smarter, prettier, or younger as to the reason that they have received something good and you didn't.

This has got to stop.

There are times when people who frequently receive good things think that there is something special about them, too. They say, 'favor isn't fair.' While that may be true for some, let me tell you what is fair, focus. Focus is an equal-opportunity manifesting tool. Fortunately for you, everyone has access to focus and favor through the C.A.R.E process. Faithful focus and appreciation for something is the key to effortlessly obtaining your desire in a way that others think there is something magical about you, there is something special about you, and there is something about you that makes you able to get into the delivery zone.

And while it is, they have to know that this is available to them, too, if they put their mind to it and submit their requisition.

ACTION STEP:

Solidify your requisition.

Start by giving yourself the freedom to have the good that you desire by making this statement: "I give myself permission to submit my requisition, to now have the perfect '____' in my life."

- **Write a detailed request**
  - What is being requested?
  - What are the specifications?
  - What is the quantity required?
  - What is the delivery date?

- **Approved!**
  - Give your request your own seal of approval.

Engage – *study to show yourself approved, to receive your desire.*

When you engage with something, you are actually becoming more familiar with it. You begin by educating yourself on the various aspects of it. For example, if you desire to be married and you educate yourself on diamonds as a part of faithfully focusing on your ideal proposal, you have to look at color, cut, and clarity. You are engaging with your dream ring. It's ok to dream big! You can scale it down later.

Remember, what you are giving faithful focus to is what you get, so the question becomes, "Am I faithfully focusing in the direction of my desire?"

What you are giving faithful focus to, is it really what you desire? Because, even if it isn't, it's what you're going to attract by simply giving your attention to it.

You have put in your requisition, now you need to engage to make sure that you are aware of how to use it when it gets to you.

Think of it like ordering a vacuum cleaner online for your dream home, and then it arrives at your home, but you don't know all of the features. You can know the basics of what you want and go ahead and request it, however, you're going to need to know what to do with it when you get it, which means you need to educate yourself on the features.

T-time: I knew to request a husband because I wanted to be a wife. But as I began to look deeper — this is really peeling back the layers within yourself — I realized I had finally made the switch from wanting to get married to desiring to be a wife to my ideal partner. For example, in the months before I started dating my husband, I chose to participate in activities that helped me to faithfully focus on becoming a wife. I even launched an exclusive virtual women's group to shift myself and other women in the group into faithfully focusing on the wife life. We completed hard and soft focused meditation and self-reflective exercises that shifted our mindset from girlfriend to wife.

I had to later ask myself, "What is it that husbands really want?" So that when my ideal partner arrives, I can give him what he desires.

The answer was simple and in the form of three "Ss": Sports, Sunday Supper, and Sex, in no particular order.

I had already put in a requisition, but I had to ask myself, "What do you need to do to prepare for this request when it is answered?"

> **Delivery zone tip:** *Your desire can absolutely show up in your delivery zone without you being prepared for it! So it's okay to request it, but then you've got to get down to the nuts and bolts of how to sustain it upon its arrival.*

You've got to immerse yourself in learning about it. So you're not surprised when it shows up and have to ask yourself, "Now what do I do?"

That's why you need to become familiar with it through the engagement process, so it's an easy and effortless transition. Because it's not wise to know you're expecting a baby and never go and prepare anything for its arrival!

There are plenty of us that ask for things but don't prepare to receive it and don't realize the consequences of approaching life in this way. That's why it's important not to put in a request for something unless you understand, at least on a basic level (and are prepared for), what's coming! Only put in a request for something that you are committed to sustaining in the future.

This is where your personal evolution starts to happen.

So supper was on my list above, and after having been single and often too busy to cook, somehow, I had figured out how to have my gourmet meals and eat them, too, without having to cook them myself. It was pretty easy. I'd just go to Central Market after work, they have all the organic dishes you could think of; the meals were freshly prepared to go. But I finally accepted that most men like a home-cooked meal at some point from their significant other. So I decided to like cooking again. I would think back to my father complimenting my cooking throughout the years as a girl learning her way around the kitchen. Or I would think about a dish that I've taken to a potluck or that I cooked for friends and received compliments. Each month, I would prepare a large family meal, pack it up in containers, and then take it to share with various friends who I either thought would enjoy it or who had especially busy weeks and could use some support.

Remember, sustaining your desire once it arrives is your responsibility.

That's why it's so important to understand that whatever you put in a request for is still up to you to take the necessary steps in getting prepared for its arrival. Are you one of those people who say, "Okay, I have put in my request, it's up to God/The Universe/My Higher Power now. It's out of my hands"? That's where people stop and wash their hands of their request, and that's why things don't always work out how they think it's going to work out.

Yes, God/The Universe/Your Higher Power is taking care of it, but you are still responsible for your part in the process.

Often, the things that we want to do the least are the things that we need to do the most in terms of our own personal transformation.

You should only ask for a garden if you intend to become a gardener and cultivate it. You have to tend to your garden. That doesn't mean you can outsource everything, either! Sure, every now and then, you may have to partner with someone to come to pull some weeds or install an irrigation system. However, you need to take full ownership of what is planted and nurtured in your garden.

Next Steps

Congratulations on getting this far!

You've done an incredible amount of work, and I'm so proud of you for keeping your commitment to the process. It can be challenging to think about pouring your faith, and sometimes your finances, into your future while remaining uncertain of your worthiness. Holding yourself accountable to the future that you are focused on is imperative. Taking the steps to bring your desired future into your current reality builds your confidence in yourself, your future, and your ability to sustain it.

Unfortunately, fear of success is as common as fear of failure. There is a lot of responsibility that goes along with maintaining the many facets of your desire once it arrives, and that can be daunting to think about.

Fear of success or failure is an internal resistance that facilitates homeostasis in your external reality.

Resistances

Homeostasis, the term from biology class, refers to the way in which your body works to maintain balance. The same is true for your external circumstances; the truth is you are more comfortable doing what you've always done than you are doing something new or different. As humans, we possess a predictable resistance to change. All resistances are an inside job and so is moving past them. In other words, resistances exist in your outer world because of your mental perception of any given situation.

On my journey to marriage, I found it most helpful to identify limiting thoughts and beliefs one by one. After identifying them, I then began challenging those views and building a belief system that was more supportive of my desire in place of the limiting ones that were being dismantled.

Resistances exist at each point of the C.A.R.E. framework and may either arise or need to be released when you are working in that area. Lets take a closer look at the resistance points that pop up at each stage of C.A.R.E.

Resistance to *characterize*

We've all had times when we've had so many goals that it was easy to become distracted by all of the decisions that needed to be made. Distractions are also a type of resistance, and in some cases, they are a choice. You can decide not to be distracted. It doesn't matter what you are occupied with; it is the fact that you are consciously or unconsciously opting not to decide on and describe your goals. Beware of multitasking, which by the way is an illusion, because you cannot consciously engage in two activities at once, unless one is on autopilot. When you are focused on setting your intentions, turn off your notifications and give it your full focus, especially in the beginning. Before starting to write this book, I disconnected from social media. At the time, I had no idea that I would get inspired to write, but the time that I spent scrolling was reallocated to time for writing. You won't always be able to connect the dots beforehand, so don't be timid about taking Divine inspired action. Remember, once you launch your desire, you will begin to receive inspiration on your next steps.

Resistance to *appreciate*

When closely examining resistances in the appreciation phase of the framework, I have found that people sometimes feel as if they don't have something to appreciate because things haven't gone exactly as they have planned in life.

They say, "Well, I don't have a good example of a healthy marriage," or "There were no married people in my life," and they end up becoming resentful instead of appreciating it wherever it can be found. So if what you desire isn't within your immediate view, then you have to go outside your comfort zone to find it and not become resentful while you are seeking a 'stand-in' to appreciate.

Resistance to *requisition*

Lack of clarity about your desire is an internal resistance. Think of the last time you needed to place an order to make a purchase but could not decide what you wanted. Right now, you are in line to receive your desired outcome but you have to know what it is first. Make sure that you are actually writing down the details of your desire. And if you receive something that you don't want, then you need to review what you actually wrote in your requisition, the actions that you took after you put in your request, and where you focused your energy after that process.

Resistance to *engage*

Subconsciously feeling helpless to connect with your desired outcome is a common hidden resistance. If, like most people, you find yourself asking, "What if there is something wrong with me? What if I am not powerful enough? What if I am not good enough to have access to this or to make this happen for myself?" That's why people, in general, say they are waiting on God because they want to believe that there is something outside of them making their dreams happen for them, as opposed to them realizing it's them co-creating the experience for themselves by tapping into the power of God within. Now take that wrinkle out of your brow while I highlight this with a very basic example. When you win a prize, you have to physically go and claim it before you can take it home. Yes, you were presented with the opportunity to win it by Divine design, but you must take action to possess it.

Post-delivery resistances

Perfection is the adversary to true fulfillment. You can combat this level of resistance by giving up thinking that your desires are going to be 100% when they come to you. Manifesting is 50-50; it is 50% manifesting your desire and 50% what you make of it after you get it. You are responsible for what you do with what you receive!

"Life begins at the end of your comfort zone."
Neale Donald Walsch

And speaking of those two sides of the same coin, cycles of success and failure are barometers for where you are on your manifestation journey. Failure lets you know how far from the mark you actually are, and success shows you a great starting point for the evolution of your desire.

The sound of your calling has to be louder than the noise in the background. Let yourself know that distractions can only defeat you if you allow them to do so. Distractions, such as others doubting your sincerity and ability to reach your goals, naysayers who don't want you to escape the potholes on the beaten path they're on, and down-right haters who just don't want to witness your happiness are common on any mission. Don't allow their negative vibes to override your positive perspective. You may find that decreasing your interaction with people who are negative minded is necessary at certain intervals. Although you cannot see this energy, it is a hidden, yet powerful, force that can slow down progression if not managed properly.

Offset this by allowing your mind and spirit to expand so that you can break the mold that has been holding you in the same place too long.

Let's examine a concept that demonstrates the power of unseen forces. Have you ever seen a wine glass shatter under the pressure of high-pitched sound vibration? Well, like you, the molecules of the wine glass are a receptacle for energy, and like your intracellular activity, they vibrate at a certain level. Those molecules and that vibration have a relationship that keeps things the way they are. When that high-pitched sound is introduced to the wine glass, it causes the glass to burst into a new state of existence.

In the very same way, that seemingly unmovable situation in your life has a relationship with your vibration. When the level of your vibration is elevated, that situation cannot hold its current state and has to expand beyond its current boundaries. This propels you into a new state of being. Hopefully, one that resonates with your desired level of happiness, marital bliss, financial abundance, etc. Like a wine glass, everything that exists resonates at a certain level and is changed by a greater vibration. Remember, all that is needed to elevate your vibration is sustained focus on something that makes you feel like you're already there. I know, you're saying if that is all, then it seems like more people would feel better right

> "Never be limited by other people's limited imaginations."
> Dr. Mae Jemison

now. Well, reigning in our focus is hard; losing it, on the other hand, is easy, really easy. Recognizing the good that is ready to emerge in your life is key to becoming your best self now. I recommend keeping a journal, a simple notebook, or even a set of notecards to write words and phrases throughout the day that keep you faithfully focused on the best and most desirable outcomes you can imagine for your life.

Success Stories

Nigel

At the end of the call I thanked him and told him how awesome he was at providing customer care. My problem had been resolved quickly and efficiently. He replied, "Thank you. I'm good at my job but I'm looking for another one. This job doesn't utilize my skills, I have two more children than I did when I got here 6 years ago, and my pay isn't enough anymore. I've been sending out my resume for over two years and have applied for 36 different positions and no one has called me back for an interview." I briefly encouraged him that the right position was out there for him and advised him to love his job like he did when he first got it by writing down one thing each day that is better about his life because of his job. I told him once his list reached 50 then he could print out a posting of his ideal position and read it daily. Before I could disconnect he said, "Wow, I could feel that you really know how to help people get unstuck. You should write a book." I then replied, "I am writing a book. It's in the editing phase now." He told me to let him know when it was ready to publish. I agreed and ended the call. A few weeks later I called the support center again and the same agent answered my call. After addressing my issue, he informed me that he had already started to implement some of the techniques I had previously shared with him and he wanted to know what to do next. He then asked for an advance copy of the book. He was sincere and motivated, so reluctantly, I shared a copy. A few months later he shared in an email that he had experienced a shift in his mindset and he felt more optimistic about his career. He stated that he had worked through his resistances and felt he was ready to engage with his ideal position. He up leveled his resume and applied for his ideal position. I received an email from him a week before publishing this book and he was excited to report that he had an interview scheduled. He expressed his gratitude and felt he could see how focusing his thoughts in the direction of his desire was impacting his situation for the better.

Michelle

When Dr. Turner first asked me to write my success story for her book I thought about all of the women over the age of 50 who needed to know that it's never too late to create your best life. Even though she is close friends with my daughter and I am friends with her mother, I always knew that what I shared with her was confidential. I went through a very difficult and public divorce from my ex-husband and the untold story is even worse than the one people knew about. I remember the day I called her for help, it was my 45th consecutive day in the house with far too many of those days spent in my bedroom, often sleeping longer than 12 hours a day. My hypersomnia was making a U-turn into insomnia and I was thinking of taking sleeping pills to lead me into eternal rest. After 57 years of living the life that most only dream about, I had hit the bottom and the rock of depression and suicidal thoughts were sitting on top of me. When she arrived for our first session I thought she was going to try to get me into a pair of my useless designer shoes and out of that big house of cards in which I was living. Instead, she brought me a hot cup of tea and handed me a dictionary and a highlighter. She reminded me that the power of life was in my mind and my mouth and told me to go through the dictionary and highlight all of the words that meant something good. Her weekly calls to check in on my progress were short, in the beginning she only asked for one word but during one of our last calls I gave her 40 words and their meaning. She never told me that I had to leave the house and get back into the swing of things but each time we spoke she would ask me where I went that day. On days that I hadn't gone anywhere she would say, "Let's go somewhere in our minds, and make it somewhere good." In hindsight I can see how she held my hand through each step in this book. She helped me C.A.R.E. again about others and more importantly about me. Living in someone else's shadow made me afraid of the light, even the light that was within me. I am now able to shine brighter than ever. I own a profitable, purpose-driven business and recently started dating a former classmate. I now have the respect of my daughters who have also found the courage to close the door to secretly abusive relationships. Rebuilding my life was difficult and I'm grateful that Dr. Turner-Wentt was there to coach me into a new reality.

Celeste

I buzzed the receptionist and told her to send up my 2pm appointment, Celeste. The young collegiate who arrived at my office was quite lovely, despite her long, messy and maybe even matted hair, her oversized black sweats that hung off her small frame, accompanied by her thick, white socks and fuzzy, black house shoes. The tears had started to well up in her eyes before I even said hello. In that session, I learned that her mother had recently insisted that she make a counseling appointment. During the summer break before her junior year of college that year, Celeste had learned that her father, a prominent public figure, had an extramarital affair.

Prior to this, she was the quintessential daddy's girl and idealized her father.

Over the following month of weekly sessions, Celeste identified that she felt let down by her father, and together, we uncovered that she also felt she was letting herself down by failing college and going to class "looking like a bum." She revealed that the sweatshirt and pants came about because her room was so chaotic that she could no longer find a complete outfit without missing class. I used that as a starting point to help her begin to C.A.R.E. I gave her an assignment to make a timeline of her relationship with her father by using pictures from her memory box.

At the end of the timeline were two simply stunning photographs of her that included her father. I wanted her to see those photos daily, so I had her remove them and place them on a separate sheet of paper along with some questions she needed to answer for the 'Celeste' in the photo. What were the dreams of the young woman in the photo? How did the Celeste in the photo feel about herself? What emotions was she experiencing in the photo? I knew the answers to these questions would cause her to hover at a much happier time in her life. She would have to think back and remember her dreams and aspirations.

One day, several months later, I buzzed the receptionist and told her to send up my 2 p.m. appointment. The young lady who arrived to at my office was quite lovely. Her long wavy tresses were expertly placed, her make-up was flawless, and she was wearing a dress that fit her form perfectly, with shoes to match. It was a complete outfit. Her mother was being honored at an event later that day, and she, her father, and brother were planning to attend together. About three- weeks after completing the assignment, Celeste was making noticeable strides toward rebuilding her faith in herself and regaining her focus on the future she desired.

If you too have experienced a challenge that's caused you to lose your faith or your focus in your desired future, I encourage you to partner with a professional who can help restore your belief in the infinite possibilities that are available to you.

WORK WITH
DR. TURNER-WENTT

When you decide to travel outside the boundaries of your current reality and into the space of unlimited possibilities you need an experienced guide to assist you on your journey.

> "We don't wait for the future, we build it."
> *Verizon*

Traneika Turner-Wentt is a counselor, consultant, and transformational teacher. She partners with men, women, couples, congregations, and companies to craft, design, and implement strategies using their *Life Logo* (shield of intention) to create their best life or an organizational atmosphere of excellence and productivity.

Full Disclosure

The intent of the author is only to offer insight and information to help you on your quest for personal growth and development.

The author of this book does not dispense medical advice or prescribe the use of any specific technique as a treatment modality for emotional, financial, or medical problems. The advice in this book does not replace a consultation with your respective advisors. Consult your qualified advisors before acting on this or any other development information. There can be no assurances that any of the results shared will be the same as your success. The author assumes no responsibility for any actions you take as a result of information provided in the book. You agree that neither the author or publisher is responsible for your decisions related to this product.

An Attitude of Gratitude

If you enjoyed this book and learned anything new from it, I'd be most grateful if you would post a brief review on Amazon. Your support matters and I personally read all the reviews so I can incorporate your feedback into making future books even better.

Moving forward

- Love and accept yourself –
  - This is the foundation for personal transformation.

- Ask with thought and feeling.
  - Use a simple statement accompanied by a feeling.

- Eliminate or neutralize low-energy thoughts.
  - Fill yourself with positivity by listening to inspirational information and reading motivational books.

- Partner with encouraging, and supportive individuals.
  - When you surround yourself with optimistic, purpose-filled people, it becomes easier to explore new possibilities.

- Stay on the path of least resistance which is gratitude.
  - Be grateful and honor yourself through each phase of your evolution.

- Last but not least, as you implement the strategies in this book, believe that you have the co-creative freedom to change your focus, control your feelings, and construct your future.

MEET THE AUTHOR

As both a licensed psychotherapist and clinical sociologist, Dr. Traneika Turner-Wentt has worked for a large academic hospital and has two decades of practice in mental healthcare and program administration. She is a transformational teacher, trendsetter, and the founder of Sacred S.P.A.C.E. Dr. Turner-Wentt has made it her life's mission to help others consciously create desirable outcomes in their personal lives. She partners with faith-based, non-profit, and for profit organizations to implement strategies and improve program effectiveness and outcomes. In her practice, Dr. Turner-Wentt conducts seminars on the transformational power of intention.

She holds a Master's degree from Smith College, a Doctorate degree in Clinical Practice and Leadership from the University of Tennessee Knoxville, and a Bachelor's degree from the University of North Texas.

When she is not reading, writing, or teaching, you can find her blending up nutritious detox smoothies. She is married to Michael Wentt, they value and prioritize family experiences and enjoy hosting and traveling with friends.

Visit *www.drturnerwentt.com* for information and updates.

REFERENCE

[1] Lisa Miller, Iris M Balodis, Clayton H McClintock, Jiansong Xu, Cheryl M Lacadie, Rajita Sinha, Marc N Potenza; Neural Correlates of Personalized Spiritual Experiences, *Cerebral Cortex*, , bhy102, https://doi.org/10.1093/cercor/bhy102

[2] Leaf C. M. Switch On Your Brain: **The Key to Peak Happiness, Thinking, and Health**. Grand Rapids, Michigan: Baker Books, 2013.

[3] "Shield." Oxford-Dictionaries.com, 2018. Web. 18 February 2018

[4] "vain." Oxford-Dictionaries.com, 2018. Web. 18 February 2018.

[5] "value." Oxford-Dictionaries.com, 2018. Web. 18 February 2018

Printed in Great Britain
by Amazon